ANTI-INFLAMMATORY COOKBOOK FOR BEGINNERS 2023

28-DAYS MEAL PLAN

1900 DAYS RECIPES

LIVIA MCDANIEL

TABLE OF CONTENT

Chapter 1:
Introductive Guide to the Anti-inflammatory Diet

ANTI-INFLAMMATORY DIET, WHAT IS IT?

Inflammation, also called inflammatory response, inflammation or inflammatory response, is a defense mechanism of the body that is activated in the presence of tissue damage of various kinds, such as, for example, damage caused by pathogens and infectious agents such as fungi, viruses, bacteria and parasites. All these factors, if not treated and treated can cause disorders and diseases.

Inflammation is a **complex physiological process,** but it is essential for our body to be able to **repair the damage caused and restore the correct functioning of the tissues and organs involved in the inflammatory process.**
Although it is a normal response that takes place to protect the body if it is not properly treated and contrasted it can cause damage and disease.
Inflammations can be of various types, but mainly acute or chronic. In the first case, it is inflammation that is limited in time, such as when you have the flu, cystitis or intestinal discomfort.

In the second case, however, we are talking about chronic inflammation, therefore a long-lasting process that can last for a long time or for life, as in the case of autoimmune diseases (rheumatoid arthritis, Hashimoto's thyroiditis, vitiligo).

In both cases, whether it is acute or chronic inflammation, it is very important to try to restore the body with an adequate anti-inflammatory diet that helps us reduce the level of inflammation.

The main purpose of the anti-inflammatory diet is to increase the molecules that help us defend ourselves against inflammation and which, at the same time, can positively affect inflammation.
In reality, there is no specific dietary program, such as the ketogenic or Mediterranean one, rather the anti-inflammatory diet consists in choosing some foods that have proven to be useful in fighting and preventing the symptoms of inflammation compared to others that seem to exacerbate the inflammation itself.

The anti-inflammatory diet is therefore to be considered as a food plan designed to reduce and minimize the effects of inflammation within our body. In fact, when our body is already fueled by inflammation mechanisms, it is very important to introduce antioxidant foods into the diet that counteract the inflammation itself.
The anti-inflammatory diet **can be very effective in counteracting inflammation caused by some chronic diseases, including type 2 diabetes mellitus, cardiovascular disease, cancer, autoimmune diseases and those related to the limbs.**

WHAT ARE THE CONSEQUENCES OF INFLAMMATION ON OUR BODY?

A lot of research has been carried out on the negative effects that inflammation can have on our bodies. Inflammations, especially if they become chronic, can lead to serious health problems such as Alzheimer's, and diabetes, but they are also the cause of overweight and obesity. Furthermore, an increase in colon cancer has been shown in people who consume only inflammatory foods. In an analysis done in 2019 and published in Clinical Nutrition, it was shown that the risk of mortality was 23% higher in people who only consumed inflammatory foods.

WHAT TO EAT AND WHAT TO AVOID IF YOU WANT TO REDUCE AND FIGHT INFLAMMATION

Selecting foods carefully is essential for an anti-inflammatory diet plan. The indications suggest moving towards the consumption of whole plant-based foods rich in healthy fats and phytonutrients, to keep glycemic values stable.
An anti-inflammatory diet, to work best, must include eight to nine servings of fruit and vegetables daily. Furthermore, the intake of red meat and dairy products with high fat content and the replacement of complex carbohydrates with whole meals and low-processed ones and the total abolition of foods with high sugar content and highly processed must be limited.

To follow an anti-inflammatory diet, you don't need to radically revolutionize the way you eat, but you need to commit to gradually changing your diet in a healthy way and correcting what has been identified as dietary errors.

A tip to always follow, for a correct anti-inflammatory diet, is to always choose foods with a high content of omega-3 fatty acids which are found mainly in fish such as anchovies, cod, hake, salmon, sardines, halibut and mussels.
On the other hand, hydrogenated fats found in seed oils, condiments and sauces that are too fatty such as mayonnaise and salad dressings, already prepared meats and fish should be avoided.

The perfect diet must therefore be based on the following food consumption:

- Fish with a high omega 3 content, and fish in general
- Fruit, especially fresh and in season
- Dried fruit
- Protein from lean meats, such as rabbit, turkey, chicken and from eggs
- Low-fat yogurt, Greek or plant-based yogurt
- Seeds and spices
- Whole meal bread, pasta and starchy foods, especially black rice
- Extra virgin olive oil
- Green tea
- Bitter cocoa
- Ginger.
- The foods to reduce are the following:
- Cereals from type 00 or 0 flours or mixtures of flours that are overly processed and with a high content of carbohydrates and sugars and low fiber content
- Packaged sweets and snacks
- Carbonated drinks and with high concentrations of sugar
- Dairy products and derivatives that are too fat
- Red meats with high fat content
- Margarine and lard.

Chapter 2:

How to Treat Inflammation Naturally

Incorrect diet and lifestyles risk triggering a series of inflammations in the body that we do not notice and which in the long run involve great health risks: with the right natural remedies, immediately turn off the inflammatory outbreaks.
If it is important to cure a disease the moment it is diagnosed, let you not forget that it is equally essential to focus on prevention.
It is now known how important it is to have a healthy and balanced diet for the proper functioning of our body. Starting from this assumption, let's see together how to orient ourselves in choosing foods that can help us prevent or, if we have already been diagnosed, counteract inflammatory diseases.

SIDE EFFECTS OF ANTI-INFLAMMATORY DRUGS

Anti-inflammatories are among the most widely used pain relievers and are almost always used to treat both mild and chronic inflammation. But they can cause side effects, even serious ones.
Choosing which drug to use to treat inflammation considers the intensity and type of pain. According to the World Health Organization (WHO) and international guidelines, there is an order of use of painkillers, which provides for the use of drugs with progressively greater analgesic power as the intensity of pain increases.

Anti-inflammatories **work by blocking the production of prostaglandins, chemical mediators of the inflammatory process.** However, prostaglandins also have other important functions in our body, and for this reason anti-inflammatories, by blocking their action, also have undesirable effects that should not be overlooked. For example, they interfere with the physiological protective mechanisms of the stomach (mediated by prostaglandins), causing anti-inflammatories to irritate our stomach and give us heartburn or stomach pains and in the worst cases, gastric-type ulcers.
Anti-inflammatories, **if taken regularly and frequently, can increase the risk of heart complications or worsen the health conditions of those who already suffer from high blood pressure.**

Another effect is that they are irritating to the stomach: between 5 and 10% of people who take anti-inflammatories regularly over a year may suffer from bleeding. Finally, diabetics should always consult their doctor before taking NSAIDs, because studies have found cases of kidney failure following their use. Furthermore, these medicines can cause allergic reactions and interfere with the action of certain antihypertensive medicines.

Corticosteroids are also among the anti-inflammatory drugs. Corticosteroids can increase your vulnerability to infection. Naturally, the extent of the risk is linked to numerous factors and in particular to the type of drug taken, the duration of treatment and the dosage.
The tablets, when taken for long periods, can cause a marked increase in appetite, muscle weakness, acne, mood changes, peptic ulcers and slowed wound healing.

Recent studies have also shown an increased risk of developing high blood pressure, diabetes, osteoporosis, cataracts and glaucoma.
If inhaled, cortisones can cause thrush inside the oral cavity, while if injected into the joints they can be the cause of swelling and acute pain.

Finally, when injected into the blood, they can cause insomnia, tachycardia and mood swings. Corticosteroids can interfere with the action of other medicines, including anticoagulants, anticonvulsants, antidiabetics, antiretrovirals, bronchodilators and some live vaccines.

NATURAL CURES

Health benefits and true gifts of nature, natural anti-inflammatories are readily available and can relieve pain and help in the event of trauma and injury.

TURMERIC

Turmeric is one of the best-known spices for its natural anti-inflammatory powers, coming from a plant that grows in Asia, particularly in Myanmar, Bangladesh, Sri Lanka and India.
This small herbaceous plant is used all over the world in the culinary field: its root is ground and dried to form a spice, recognizable by its bright color.
Turmeric is now considered one of the most antioxidant plants in the world, thanks to its composition of curcumins and curcuminoids. **It contains essential oils and starch but, that's not all: turmeric also contains vitamin B6 in interesting quantities, as well as vitamins C, E, K, B1 and B2.**
In turmeric, we also find some mineral salts and trace elements, such as zinc, magnesium, iron, copper, manganese, phosphorus and potassium.
It is to this composition that we owe the many properties of turmeric, including its very powerful anti-inflammatory virtues.

FENUGREEK

Fenugreek is a plant native to the Middle and Near East: it is found in India, Egypt and throughout the Mediterranean basin. Its leaves are used in various ways, including as a dried herb. The seeds of the plant are ground into a spice, often combined in blends such as pigeon or caraway.
Fenugreek has a surprising composition: the seeds of the plant contain 10% fat, 20% carbohydrates and 30% protein. They also contain various nutrients, such as vitamins **(A, C and B1)**, as well as various mineral salts: sulfur, calcium, iron, and magnesium. What distinguishes fenugreek from other spices is its high content of phosphorus, amino acids and saponins.
This plant and its seeds are also rich in flavonoids (which are antioxidants), essential oils, mucilaginous fibers, lecithin, and alkaloids.
Fenugreek has been used for ages to treat and relieve inflammation of the skin, as well as nerve pain and rheumatism.
Fenugreek seeds are ground into powder and used as a compressor as a food supplement.

GINGER

Ginger, famous for its numerous virtues, is one of the best natural anti-inflammatory drugs that can be used.
Its composition includes gingerol, an active ingredient known to act on inflammation sites in the human body. This root also contains antioxidants and vitamins **(mainly A, provitamin A and B9).**
In its composition, there are also mineral salts and trace elements: calcium, iodine, magnesium, manganese, copper, phosphorus, selenium, potassium and sodium.
In humans, ginger consumption can relieve arthritis and pain associated with chronic inflammatory disorders. It can therefore be interesting to consume ginger as a food supplement, as an infusion, as a spice or simply in its natural form.

WHITE WILLOW

White willow is also among the best natural anti-inflammatory drugs. This plant comes from the Willow family: it is a dioecious tree that grows in the wetlands of Europe. Its branches provide wicker, and its bark is removed from two to three-year-old branches for medicinal use.
It has been used for centuries in Greek and Chinese medicine to treat all types of inflammation.
White willow contains flavonoids (luteolin, naringenin, quercetol heterosides, eriodictyol), tannins, phenolic compounds and salicylates.
White willow bark is best known for relieving lower back pain and reducing the use of conventional medications. Additionally, several studies have determined that white willow can treat osteoarthritis as well. White willow extract has been shown to be as effective as anti-inflammatory drugs in reducing pain in the hip and knee. Finally, white willow bark can also relieve rheumatoid arthritis in people who suffer from it.

THE HARPAGOPHYTUM OR DEVIL'S CLAW

This root, commonly known among natural anti-inflammatories as "devil's claw", has its origins in Africa. It grows mainly in Angola, Namibia, Botswana and southern Africa. Its medicinal properties have only recently been discovered, during the 20th century, and science has become very interested in its anti-inflammatory powers, comparing them with the effects of ibuprofen. Devil's claw contains a wide variety of vitamins, including **vitamin B (B1, B2, B3, B5, B9 and B12), vitamin C and beta-carotene, in small amounts.** The root also contains various mineral salts, including phosphorus, calcium, copper, magnesium, iron, potassium and silica.
Most of the benefits of devil's claw are related to its active ingredients, including harpagoside, flavonoids, phenols, chlorogenic acid and cinnamic acid.

Chapter 3:

The Importance of the Anti-Inflammatory Diet in Managing Arthritis, Inflammation & Chronic Pain

Many studies have been done in favor of the inflammation-nutrition association. In an article published in Frontiers in Nutrition, dated November 2017, it was also shown that taking anti-inflammatory foods reduced the symptoms of rheumatoid arthritis in subjects participating in a scientific study. In particular, the authors of this study have shown that following a type of diet mainly based on fruit and vegetables has reduced the progression of the disease not only that, but they have also reduced the joint damage caused by the disease and the dependence on drugs used for therapy.

Another study carried out in 2020 showed how some people suffering from arthritic knee disorders responded positively to a diet containing high concentrations of antioxidants and flavonoids.
Since the joints are the point where our body accumulates not only free radicals but also uric acid, it is essential to follow a lifestyle that deacidifies the body starting with a healthy diet.

The role of diet and exercise is essential to be able to fight not only osteoarthritis but also inflammation and chronic pain.

For this reason, it is necessary to follow some fundamental steps that can help you manage the situation:

- Always try to keep your weight under control, trying to stay in the appropriate body mass range for your age and height. Furthermore, this concept is essential if you suffer from osteoarthritis as the excessive weight will only further overload your joints. Choosing a diet rich in anti-inflammatory foods can help reduce the symptoms of arthritis, while also reducing the risk factors and consequences of the disease such as swelling.

- It is important to reduce salt and try to replace it with condiments like ginger, chili, curry, sage, rosemary, fennel seeds and cumin seeds.

- Consume foods rich in vitamins and mineral salts, especially vitamin c and vitamin d, beta-carotenes and fatty acids.

- Eat a healthy, nutritious diet made up mostly of wholesome foods such as fruits and vegetables.

- It is useful to include a minimum of 2-3 servings of oily fish per week in the diet. Fish oil supplements can also be a solution. There is a wide variety of fish oil supplements, which is why it can be helpful to seek advice from a dietician or doctor before taking large doses of fish oil supplements. Evidence suggests that 3,000 mg of omega-3s over a 3-month period helps reduce pain, especially in rheumatoid arthritis. Fish oil supplements contain a combination of EPA and DHA (two types of omega-3s). It is important to ensure that the EPA/DHA ratio is ≥1.5. Therefore, if you decide to use fish oil supplements, a good quality brand that contains a high dose of omega-3s is important. Dried fruit, especially walnuts, flax and chia seeds are also a good source of omega-3s and an intake of 30 g per day is recommended.

- Increase your fiber intake. Fiber is important for proper digestion and maintaining a healthy microbiome, as well as weight management. When you increase your fiber intake, it's important to increase your fluid intake as well. Fiber and fluids work together to promote gut health. The microbiota, i.e., the set of all the bacteria that make up the gastrointestinal tract, plays an important role in stress and in the onset of gastrointestinal disorders. An imbalance between these bacteria can lead to a condition called "dysbiosis", which can give rise to various diseases, including metabolic syndrome or irritable bowel syndrome, which involves visceral pain, swelling and changes in bowel habits.

- Give due importance to rest. If you suffer from inflammation or joint pain, resting well and for the right amount of time is essential to ensure a good quality of life.

Furthermore, an adequate diet can have positive effects on chronic pain for several reasons:

- Nutrition can improve the functionality of the nervous, immune and endocrine systems, directly influencing pain management.
- Diet and body weight affect the risk and/or severity of other chronic diseases that often co-occur with chronic pain and make it worse.

Chapter 4:
Recipes

Alaska Pollock & Pumpkin Soup

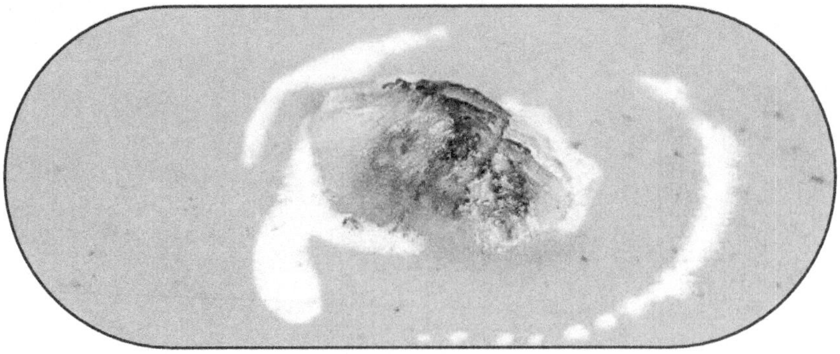

Preapering	Servings	Cooking	Calories
15 Minutes	2 People	20 Minutes	230

Ingredients:

- 10.5 oz of pumpkin pulp
- 14 oz of Alaska Pollock fillet
- 2 tsp of fresh chopped thyme
- 1 tsp of chopped bay leaves
- 1 tsp of minced ginger
- 1 chopped chipotle

Nutritional Values:

Carb:	11 Gr.
Proteins:	25 Gr.
Fats:	8 Gr.

Steps for Cooking:

1. As the first step, peel and wash a piece of onion and then chop it thinly.
2. Wash and dry the chipotle and then chop it as well.
3. Peel the pumpkin, eliminate the seeds, and remove only the pulp. Than wash the pumpkin pulp and then split it into cubes.
4. Wash and dry the thyme, bay and ginger, so mince them together and put some olive oil in a pan..
5. Once hot enough, brown the piece of onion and the mix of herbs and ginger.
6. Now join the pumpkin cubes and chipotle to them and sauté for 15 minutes.
7. Sauté for 15 minutes, season with salt and pepper, add some water and keep on cooking for another 15 minutes.
8. Now, clean the Alaska Pollock fillet, wash it and slice it.
9. Now pour the contents of the pan into the pan with the sliced Alaska Pollock fillet.
10. Proceed with the cooking for another 10/12 minutes.

Almond & Pecans Carrot Cream

Preapering	Servings	Cooking	Calories
15 Minutes	2 People	0 Minutes	150

Ingredients:

- 2 big size carrot
- Juice of one lemon
- ½ cup of sugar free oat milk
- 2 cups of cold vegetable broth
- Crushed almonds and pecans

Nutritional Values:

Carb:	13 Gr.
Proteins:	5 Gr.
Fats:	10 Gr.

Steps for Cooking:

1. First, peel the carrot, wash and mince. Chop a piece of shallot too.
2. Transfer all ingredients (carrots, shallots, lemon juice, oat milk, vegetable broth, salt, and pepper into a measuring cup).
3. Put it to rest in the fridge for about 20 minutes.
4. After this time, take the ingredients and blend them with an immersion blender.
5. Season the carrot cream with salt and sprinkle with the almonds and walnuts.
6. You can serve your carrot and nuts cream with croutons of wholemeal bread.

Avocado & Turkey Garam Masala Soup

Preapering	Servings	Cooking	Calories
15 Minutes	2 People	45 Minutes	270

Ingredients:

- 1 cup of cubed turkey breast
- ½ avocado
- 1 tsp of ginger powder
- 1 tsp of chopped chipotle
- 1 tsp of Garam Masala
- 1 tsp of chopped bay leaves

Nutritional Values:

Carb:	4 Gr.
Proteins:	25 Gr.
Fats:	19 Gr.

Steps for Cooking:

1. Start this recipe by washing the half avocado, pitting it and then dividing it into cubes.
2. Rinse, clean and cube the turkey breast too.
3. So, pour a tablespoon of olive oil into a saucepan and, once it will be hot, add the avocado cubes and bay leaves.
4. Stir, cook for a couple of minutes and then add the turkey cubes. Sauté them for 10 minutes, then add pepper, salt, chopped chipotle, ginger and Garam Masala powder.
5. Keep on cooking all these ingredients, adding two glasses of water. Let boil and proceed with the cooking for 10 minutes.
6. Once the spicy avocado and turkey Garam Masala soup is cooked, turn it off and place it on serving dishes. Sprinkle with raw oil, and chopped parsley and serve.

Cabbage & Radicchio Turmeric Soup

Preapering	Servings	Cooking	Calories
15 Minutes	2 People	90 Minutes	170

Ingredients:

- 2 eggs
- ½ cup of green cabbage
- 3.5 oz of radicchio
- 1 sprig of rosemary
- 2 sage leaves
- A pinch of turmeric powder

Nutritional Values:

Carb:	5 Gr.
Proteins:	13 Gr.
Fats:	12 Gr.

Steps for Cooking:

1. First, wash and dry the green cabbage, taking only the inner leaves and removing the outer ones. Take the leaves and cut them into very small pieces.
2. Also, wash the radicchio leaves, dry them and cut them into small pieces and wash and dry rosemary and sage.
3. Put the olive oil in a saucepan to heat and add the sage and rosemary, fry for a minute and then add both the radicchio and the cabbage.
4. Cook for 5 minutes and then add a liter of hot water. Add salt, pepper and turmeric powder.
5. Put the lid on and cook over medium heat for 60 minutes, stirring occasionally.
6. Once the vegetables are done, go on to prepare the eggs.
7. Take a pan and put a liter of water and the vinegar.
8. Bring the water to a boil. When the water boils, slide an egg into the water and cook it for 3 minutes trying not to break it.
9. The eggs should be placed directly into the plate with the soup, so while the egg is cooking, divide the anti-inflammatory soup between two serving plates. You can serve.

Cannellini Beans & Hake Soup

Preapering	Servings	Cooking	Calories
10 Minutes	2 People	20 Minutes	250

Ingredients:

- 1 cup of cubed hake fillet
- 1 cup of already soaked and boiled cannellini beans
- 1 tbsp of chopped marjoram
- 1 tsp of cumin powder
- 1 tsp of chopped coriander leaves

Nutritional Values:

Carb:	25 Gr.
Proteins:	22 Gr.
Fats:	6 Gr.

Steps for Cooking:

1. First, wash and dry the hake cubes (after having eliminated all the bones) and let drain.
2. Rinse and drain the boiled cannellini beans.
3. So, peel a piece of onion and then mince it and wash and dry both marjoram and coriander leaves.
4. Now, you should heat up a bit of olive oil in a saucepan and once hot enough, fry the and onion.
5. After 3 minutes, add the coriander and cannellini beans, mix and sauté for the other 2 minutes.
6. Now add the marjoram, and hake cubes, season with salt, cumin powder and pepper and sauté for 5 minutes.
7. So, join three cups of water with these ingredients and bring them to a boil.
8. Keep on cooking for 15 minutes, cover all with the lid above and then switch off.
9. Put the hake and cannellini beans soup on serving plates, season with a drizzle of oil and serve still hot.

Chickpea Chili Turkey Cream Soup

Preapering	Servings	Cooking	Calories
20 Minutes	2 People	120 Minutes	290

Ingredients:

- 1 cup of already-cleaned turkey breast
- 7 oz of already boiled chickpeas
- 1 tsp of chopped chili
- ½ glass of apple cider vinegar
- 1 tbsp of chopped mint leaves

Nutritional Values:

Carb:	34 Gr.
Proteins:	15 Gr.
Fats:	3 Gr.

Steps for Cooking:

1. Start this anti-inflammatory recipe by rinsing the already cleaned (fat and skinless) turkey breast under running water, let it drain and splitting it into cubes.
2. Now, you can peel and wash a piece of onion and then chop it.
3. Heat the olive oil in a saucepan and, once hot enough, arrange the onion and chili pepper to sauté for 1 minute and, after this operation, put the turkey meat cubes.
4. Cook for 6 minutes.
5. Now add a glass of hot water, and apple cider vinegar and cook for another 10 minutes.
6. Let it evaporate and join the chickpeas to the turkey.
7. Cook for another 4/5 minutes and season with salt and pepper.
8. So, after cooking time, switch off and let all the anti-inflammatory ingredients rest for two minutes.
9. Now put the turkey and chickpeas soup on the plates, season it with a bit of olive oil, sprinkle with chopped mint leaves and serve.

Cinnamon, Turmeric & Squid Soup

Preapering	Servings	Cooking	Calories
15 Minutes	2 People	15 Minutes	110

Ingredients:

- 1 cup of squid rings
- 1 cup of vegetable stock
- 1 tsp of ground cinnamon
- 1 tsp of chopped cilantro

Nutritional Values:

Carb:	2 Gr.
Proteins:	14 Gr.
Fats:	2 Gr.

Steps for Cooking:

1. Start this soup anti-inflammatory recipe by rinsing the squid rings and letting them drain.
2. Peel a piece of scallion, so mince it.
3. Heat a bit of oil in a saucepan and, once it is hot, brown the scallion pieces.
4. Once it will turn golden, add the ground cinnamon and vegetable stock and bring to a boil.
5. Flavor with salt and pepper and then add the squid rings.
6. Keep on cooking for 10 minutes and then switch it off.
7. So, pour the rings and cinnamon soup into two serving plates, sprinkle with the chopped cilantro leaves and serve.

Lentils & Tilapia Soup

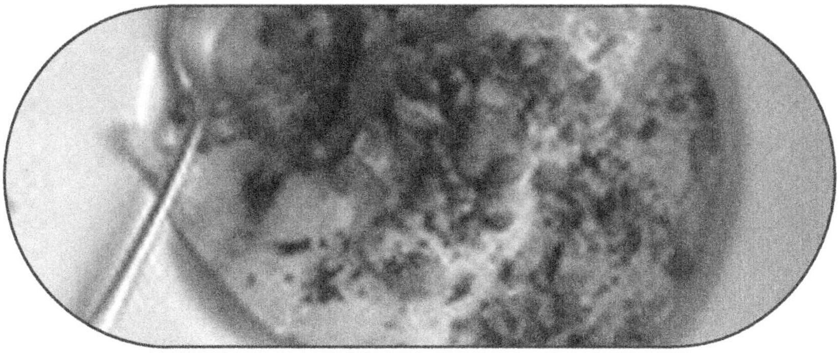

Preapering	Servings	Cooking	Calories
15 Minutes	2 People	20 Minutes	260

Ingredients:

- 1 cup and ½ of tilapia fillet
- ½ cup of already-soaked lentils
- 1 spring onion
- 1 small carrot
- 3 cups of vegetable stock
- 1 tsp of chopped chipotle

Nutritional Values:

Carb:	10 Gr.
Proteins:	21 Gr.
Fats:	3 Gr.

Steps for Cooking:

1. The first operation for this anti-inflammatory recipe: let the vegetable stock heat up in a pan; meanwhile, wash and dry the chipotle, so chop it.
2. Peel the carrot and spring onion, wash them and then chop finely. Than rinse the soaked lentils under running water and then leave them to drain.
3. Wash and dry the tilapia fillet, after having eliminated all the present bones, and then cube the fish.
4. Heat a little olive oil in a saucepan and then brown the pieces of carrot spring onions. Add the chopped chipotle too.
5. So, cook for 2 minutes, add the tilapia cubes and sauté for 5 minutes. Than add the lentils and mix.
6. Sauté for 5 minutes, so coat everything with the hot vegetable stock.
7. Boil the lentil and tilapia soup, adding salt and pepper for 40 minutes.
8. After this time, remove the tilapia fillet and keep it aside. Than continue cooking the lentils for another 15/20 minutes.
9. After this time, switch off and pour the lentils and the broth onto serving plates.
10. Add the tilapia cubes and serve.

Porcini & Ginger Soy Cheese Curry

Preapering	Servings	Cooking	Calories
15 Minutes	2 People	20 Minutes	180

Ingredients:

- 1/3 cup of soy cheese
- ¼ cup of porcini mushrooms
- 1 piece of chopped fresh ginger
- 1 cup of vegetable broth
- 1 garlic clove
- 2 teaspoons of curry powder

Nutritional Values:

Carb:	3 Gr.
Proteins:	22 Gr.
Fats:	2 Gr.

Steps for Cooking:

1. The first step of the recipe: peel and wash the garlic, then mince it.
2. Take away the earthy part from the porcini mushrooms, wash them, dry them and cut them into slices.
3. Take a piece of ginger, peel it and then chop it. Than rinse and pat the soy cheese dry with paper towels and then cut it into cubes.
4. Heat a spoonful of olive oil in a pan and, as soon as it is hot, brown the garlic.
5. Now add the sliced mushrooms, mix and brown them for a couple of minutes.
6. Now add the vegetable broth and minced ginger and cook for another 5 minutes, then add the soy cheese, curry, salt and pepper and mix.
7. Cover the pan and cook for another 10 minutes.
8. After 10 minutes, switch off and put the soy cheese and mushrooms on serving plates.
9. Sprinkle with the cooking liquid and the chopped cilantro leaves and serve.

Scallops & Chili Pepper Sauce Penne

Preapering	Servings	Cooking	Calories
15 Minutes	2 People	35 Minutes	415

Ingredients:

- ½ cup and 2 tbsp of wholemeal penne
- 2 cups of shelled scallops
- ½ glass of apple cider vinegar
- 4 chopped cilantro leaves
- 1/3 cup of tomato pulp
- 1 tsp of chili pepper (chopped)

Nutritional Values:

Carb:	49 Gr.
Proteins:	23 Gr.
Fats:	8 Gr.

Steps for Cooking:

1. As the first step for this recipe, arrange a pot of water and salt on the fire and wait for boiling. Than peel and wash a piece of scallion and then chop it.
2. Rinse the shelled scallops under running water and then let them drain.
3. So, heat a bit of olive oil in a pan. Once quite hot, put the onion piece and chili pepper to brown.
4. Now add the scallops, mix, and sauté for 2 minutes.
5. Add the apple cider vinegar and let it evaporate. At this point, you may add the 1/3 cup of tomato pulp and cook for 15 minutes about.
6. After this time indicated, season with salt and pepper and turn off.
7. When the water is boiling, pour in the pasta, and cook for 10/12 minutes.
8. When the penne will be cooked, drain, and pour them into the pan with the scallop and chili sauce.
9. Put together well and then put the scallops sauce pasta on serving plates and serve.

Turmeric & Pistachio Chicken Brown Rice

Preapering	Servings	Cooking	Calories
15 Minutes	2 People	40 Minutes	510

Ingredients:

- 5.7 oz of brown rice
- 5.7 oz of chicken breast
- 2 tbsp of chopped pistachios
- Half an orange
- 1 tsp of turmeric powder

Nutritional Values:

Carb:	45 Gr.
Proteins:	38 Gr.
Fats:	10 Gr.

Steps for Cooking:

1. The first step of the recipe: clean, and slice the turkey breast, so place these meat slices in a bowl, along with the filtered half orange juice, turmeric powder, salt, pepper and a bit of olive oil.
2. Let the chicken marinate for 20 minutes.
3. So, in the meantime, heat the water, salt, and pepper in a saucepan and bring to a boil. Once it's boiling, arrange the brown rice, and let it cook for 25 minutes.
4. Once cooked, drain the brown rice and transfer it to a bowl.
5. Now, put a tablespoon of oil in a pan and brown 1 tbsp of chopped onion for a couple of minutes. Add the turmeric-marinated chicken with all the marinating liquid. Stir and cook for another 15 minutes.
6. Put the turmeric and orange chicken with all the cooking juices in the bowl with the rice. Add the chopped almonds and mix all the ingredients well.
7. Put the anti- inflammatory rice and chicken on the serving plates and serve.

Zucchini & Oat Creamy Soup

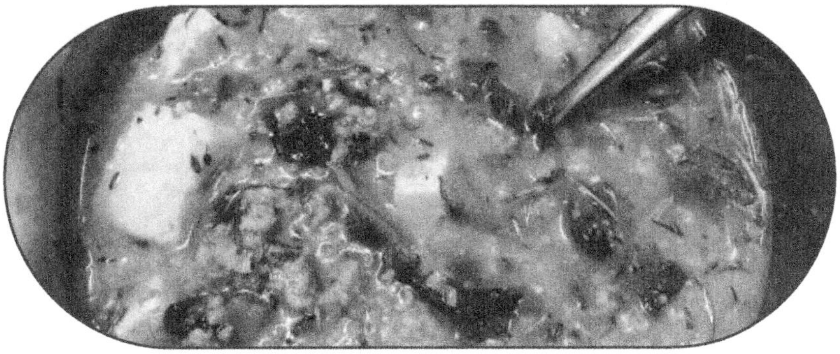

Preapering	Servings	Cooking	Calories
20 Minutes	2 People	15 Minutes	90

Ingredients:

- 1 cup and ½ of zucchini
- 2 tablespoons of oat flour
- 2 bay leaves
- 1 sprig of rosemary
- 3 cups of hot vegetable stock
- 1 pinch of nutmeg

Nutritional Values:

Carb:	16 Gr.
Proteins:	5 Gr.
Fats:	2 Gr.

Steps for Cooking:

1. As the first step, peel the zucchini. So, rinse them under running water and then split them into cubes.
2. Now, you can heat 2 tbsp of olive oil in a saucepan.
3. Once hot enough, add the oat flour and toast it for 2/3 minutes.
4. Add the cups of vegetable stock and stir continuously with a manual whisk.
5. Now you can add the other ingredients: zucchini, rosemary, bay, a pinch of nutmeg, salt, and pepper.
6. Keep cooking for another 15 minutes, stirring occasionally.
7. After 15 minutes, turn off and put the zucchini and nutmeg soup on serving plates.
8. Season with a little oil and serve this anti-inflammatory dish.

Avocado & Porcini Mushrooms Halibut

Preapering	Servings	Cooking	Calories
25 Minutes	2 People	12 Minutes	340

Ingredients:

- 14 oz of halibut fillet
- 10.5 oz of porcini mushrooms
- ½ avocado
- 1 tbsp chopped cilantro
- 1 tbsp of chopped pine nuts

Nutritional Values:

Carb:	5 Gr.
Proteins:	32 Gr.
Fats:	16 Gr.

Steps for Cooking:

1. Start this halibut recipe by eliminating the stem and earthy parts from the mushrooms well by then spilled into slices.
2. Peel 1 tbsp of onion and cut it into slices. Than peel and pit the half avocado, so divide the pulp into some pieces.
3. So, brush, at this point, a baking tray with olive oil. Than remove the bone from the halibut fillet, cut it into 4 slices and put it in the baking pan.
4. Place the avocado pieces in the baking pan with the halibut.
5. Add the sliced porcini mushrooms and flavor everything with oil, salt and pepper.
6. Sprinkle with the onion and chopped pine nuts and place the plaice in the oven. Cook at 392°F for 12 minutes, turning the place halfway through cooking.
7. After 12 minutes, remove the halibut from the oven and arrange it on two plates.
8. Add the porcini mushroom slices and avocado and serve.

Black Cabbage & Almond Trout Stew

Preapering	Servings	Cooking	Calories
25 Minutes	2 People	20 Minutes	370

Ingredients:

- 1 cup and 2 tbsp of trout fillet
- 1 cup of black cabbage leaves
- 1 tsp of chopped coriander
- 2 cups of fish broth
- 1 tsp of chili powder

Nutritional Values:

Carb:	4 Gr.
Proteins:	35 Gr.
Fats:	16 Gr.

Steps for Cooking:

1. The first thing to do is wash the coriander and transfer it to a pan.
2. Add the chopped onion and a drizzle of oil and heat up.
3. Now add the fish broth and boil.
4. So, rinse the black cabbage leaves with running water and divide them into small pieces.
5. Take these cabbage pieces and transfer them to the pot with the boiling fish broth.
6. Cook for another 10 minutes, then add the cleaned diced trout fillet.
7. Flavor with salt and pepper, add the chili powder put the lid on the pan and cook for 15 minutes.
8. After 15 minutes, switch off and put the stew on two plates, covering it with the cooking juices and chopped cilantro leaves.
9. You can serve this trout and cilantro anti-inflammatory stew.

Chia Seeds & Mustard Plaice

Preapering	Servings	Cooking	Calories
10 Minutes	2 People	20 Minutes	330

Ingredients:

- 2 plaice fillets (7 oz for each)
- 2 tsp of chia seeds
- 2 tbsp of mustard sauce
- 1 lime
- 1 tsp of turmeric powder

Nutritional Values:

Carb:	8 Gr.
Proteins:	29 Gr.
Fats:	7 Gr.

Steps for Cooking:

1. As a first step for this recipe, mix the mustard with the lime juice, 2 tsp of olive oil, the soy sauce, the turmeric powder, and a pinch of salt and pepper in a bowl.
2. Put the cleaned plaice fillet in a baking dish and sprinkle it with the mustard lime sauce. Marinate for 20 minutes at least, turning the plaice often.
3. After this time, sprinkle the plaice fillet with the 2 tsp chia seeds.
4. Arrange the plaice in a baking pan that you will bring in the oven and cook at 338°F for 20 minutes.
5. After 20 minutes, take the chia seeds plaice fillet out of the oven and put it on the plates.
6. Sprinkle the plaice with the rest of the lime and mustard sauce and serve.

Chipotle & Roasted Chicken Stuffed Avocado

Preapering	Servings	Cooking	Calories
15 Minutes	2 People	0 Minutes	320

Ingredients:

- 1 ripe big size avocado
- ½ cup of roasted chicken
- 1 ripe tomato
- Chopped walnuts

Nutritional Values:

Carb:	5 Gr.
Proteins:	38 Gr.
Fats:	16 Gr.

Steps for Cooking:

1. As the first step, wash and dry the avocado, cut it in half and pit it.
2. Take away the pitted pulp from the avocado with the help of a spoon and put it in a bowl.
3. Now, rinse the ripe tomato, cut it into cubes and transfer it to the bowl with the avocado pulp.
4. Cut the roasted chicken into small pieces and place in the bowl with the avocado pulp and tomato.
5. Add a bit of lemon juice, salt, pepper, mustard sauce and a little oil and mix well.
6. So, place the filled avocado on two plates and add the filling.
7. Sprinkle with chopped walnuts and serve.

Carrot & Peas Turkey

Preapering	Servings	Cooking	Calories
20 Minutes	2 People	15 Minutes	390

Ingredients:

- 2 turkey breasts, 1 cup about for each
- 2.5 oz of fresh shelled peas
- 1 diced carrot
- 1 pinch of curry powder
- Vegetable broth to taste

Nutritional Values:

Carb:	12 Gr.
Proteins:	57 Gr.
Fats:	9 Gr.

Steps for Cooking:

1. So, start with washing the 2 turkey breasts and pat them dry with a paper towel, then split it into four parts.
2. Heat 1 tsp of oil in a pan and then put the turkey parts. Le the meat cooks for 3 minutes on each side.
3. Wash the carrot, and dice and put them in the pan with the turkey meat.
4. Join the rinsed and drained peas to the turkey. So, season your ingredients with salt, curry powder, and pepper.
5. Add 2 glasses of hot vegetable stock and cook for 15 minutes, checking the cooking and stirring turkey and veggies occasionally.
6. After 15 minutes, turn off the heat and divide the turkey, peas and carrots into two plates and serve.

Cauliflower, Pink Pepper & Ginger Salmon

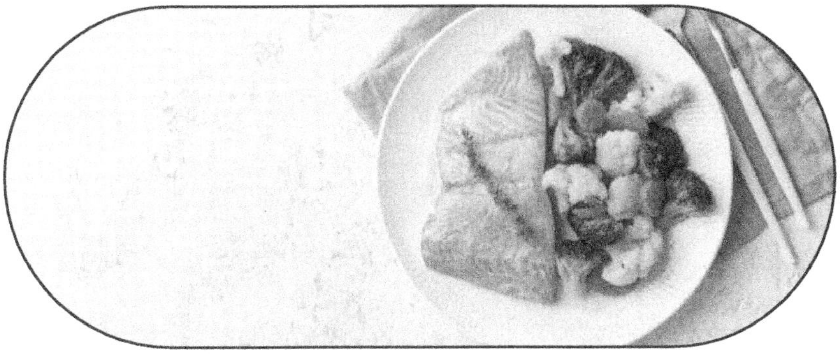

Preapering	Servings	Cooking	Calories
5 Minutes	2 People	10 Minutes	350

Ingredients:

- 2 cups of salmon fillet
- 1 cup of cauliflower tops
- 1 tsp of ginger powder
- 1 tsp of pink peppercorns
- ½ orange juice

Nutritional Values:

Carb:	5 Gr.
Proteins:	36 Gr.
Fats:	14 Gr.

Steps for Cooking:

1. The first thing of all: wash and dry the flowers of the cauliflower, so split them into many pieces.
2. Remove any excess bones from the salmon, then wash and dry it.
3. Wash and dry a sage leaf.
4. Now place the olive oil, orange juice, pink peppercorns, salt, ginger powder, and pepper in a small bowl and stir these ingredients with a fork until you get a thick emulsion.
5. Take one sheet of aluminum foil and arrange the cleaned salmon fillet. Add the cauliflower, and sage leaf and then sprinkle with the orange and pink pepper emulsion.
6. So, now you can close the foil, sealing it well.
7. Place in the oven and bake the salmon at 392°F for 15 minutes.
8. Once ready, remove the sage leaf and serve the salmon fillet with the cauliflower and sprinkled it with the marinating liquid.

Coconut Milk & Yellow Tomato Chicken

Preapering	Servings	Cooking	Calories
20 Minutes	2 People	20 Minutes	290

Ingredients:

- 2 chicken breasts (7 oz for each)
- 6 yellow cherry tomatoes
- ½ cup of coconut milk
- 2 tbsp of fresh pineapple juice
- 1 tsp of cumin powder

Nutritional Values:

Carb:	10 Gr.
Proteins:	52 Gr.
Fats:	8 Gr.

Steps for Cooking:

1. As the first step for this meat recipe, peel the garlic clove and cut it into thin slices.
2. Wash the yellow tomatoes and cut them into slices as well.
3. Eliminate the fat from the chicken, wash and dry it and brown the breasts for 3 minutes in a pan.
4. Turn the chicken meat, so you can add the sliced garlic and tomatoes and cook for another 5 minutes.
5. Now add the pineapple juice, the tsp of cumin powder, coconut milk, salt and pepper and cook for 10 minutes.
6. Now coat the chicken with the lid and keep on cooking for another 6 minutes.
7. After 6 minutes have passed, turn off and put the chicken, garlic and yellow tomatoes on the plates.
8. Sprinkle with the coconut pineapple cooking sauce and serve this anti-inflammatory meat recipe.

Fennel Seeds & Asparagus Alaska Pollock Cubes

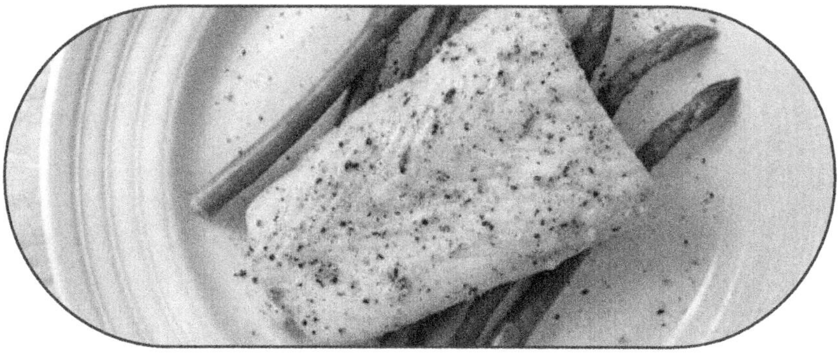

Preapering	Servings	Cooking	Calories
30 Minutes	2 People	15 Minutes	250

Ingredients:

- 14 oz of cubed Alaska Pollock fillet
- 14 oz of asparagus
- ¼ cup orange juice
- 1 tbsp of fennel seeds
- Olive oil to taste

Nutritional Values:

Carb:	7 Gr.
Proteins:	28 Gr.
Fats:	5 Gr.

Steps for Cooking:

1. As the first step for this recipe, eliminate the stem and the hardest part of the asparagus.
2. Rinse them under running water and then blanch for 10 minutes in boiling salted water.
3. Meanwhile, wash and dry the Alaska Pollock fillet and then cut it into cubes.
4. After boiling time, drain the asparagus and set them aside.
5. Heat a bit of oil in a pan and then put the Alaska Pollock cubes to sauté.
6. Join the filtered orange juice to the fish, season with salt and pepper and cook for 8/10 minutes.
7. Now add the asparagus and fennel seeds too, stir, cook well and switch off the heat.
8. Put the Alaska Pollock and asparagus on serving plates, sprinkle with the fennel seeds cooking juices and serve.

Coriander & Onion Tuna

Preapering	Servings	Cooking	Calories
15 Minutes	2 People	10 Minutes	272

Ingredients:

- 1 tuna fillet (10.5 oz about)
- 1 tbsp of Olive Oil
- 1 tbsp of chopped onion
- ¼ tsp of onion Powder
- 1 tbsp of chopped coriander

Nutritional Values:

Carb:	2 Gr.
Proteins:	29 Gr.
Fats:	13 Gr.

Steps for Cooking:

1. First, wash and let dry the already cleaned tuna fillet. Than brush the tuna fillet with some olive oil.
2. Sprinkle one side with salt, pepper, and onion powder.
3. Place the tuna fillet sprinkled with chopped onion in the baking pan.
4. Preheat your oven to 338°F.
5. Once this temperature arrives let cook the onion tuna for 7 minutes.
6. Then flip the tuna fillet over and cook for another 8 minutes.
7. Check the tuna cooking and if you are not satisfied, keep it for 3 minutes.
8. Meanwhile, wash and dry the coriander.
9. Serve the onion tuna immediately, hot, with the just chopped coriander.

Fenugreek Seeds & Marjoram Mackerel

Preapering	Servings	Cooking	Calories
10 Minutes	2 People	5 Minutes	190

Ingredients:

- 7 oz of sliced mackerel fillet
- 1 tbsp of fresh chopped marjoram
- 1 tsp of fenugreek seeds powder
- 1 tsp of lime zest

Nutritional Values:

Carb:	2 Gr.
Proteins:	24 Gr.
Fats:	10 Gr.

Steps for Cooking:

1. First, rinse the already cleaned mackerel fillet (skinless and boneless) and let it drain, so slice.
2. Meanwhile, wash and chop the tbsp of marjoram leaves.
3. Season the mackerel slices with salt and pepper.
4. Join the fenugreek seeds powder and chopped marjoram with the sliced mackerel.
5. Place the mackerel slices in a baking tray and sprinkle them with olive oil and grate the zest of a lime on top.
6. So, let cook the marjoram mackerel in the oven at 392° F for 12/13 minutes.
7. Serve this mackerel and fenugreek seeds dish while still hot.

Cucumber & Soy Basil Sauce Hake

Preapering	Servings	Cooking	Calories
15 Minutes	2 People	10 Minutes	260

Ingredients:

- 2 fresh hake fillets, 7 oz each
- 1 cucumber
- 8 basil leaves
- 2 tbsp of already chopped pine nuts
- 2 tsp of grated soy cheese

Nutritional Values:

Carb:	7 Gr.
Proteins:	32 Gr.
Fats:	7 Gr.

Steps for Cooking:

1. Start this recipe, by preparing the soy cheese and basil sauce.
2. So, arrange the basil leaves, grated soy cheese, pine nuts, salt, pepper and 3 tsp of olive oil in a blender, so mince everything until you obtain a sort of "pesto".
3. So, clean, eliminate the bones, and wash the hake fillets and transfer them to a pan with a drizzle of hot oil.
4. Cook the hake fillets for 3/4 minutes on each side.
5. Once cooked, place the just cooked hake fillets on a cutting board and divide them into some slices.
6. Peel the cucumber now, divide it into thin slices and place it into two plates.
7. Put the hake slices on top, sprinkle with the pesto soy sauce and serve.

Garam Masala & Almond Milk Tuna

Preapering	Servings	Cooking	Calories
35 Minutes	2 People	15 Minutes	350

Ingredients:

- 14 oz of tuna fillet
- 1 tsp of Garam Masala
- ½ cup of almond milk
- 1 tbsp of fresh pineapple juice
- 1 chopped spring onion
- 1 tbsp of chopped fresh marjoram

Nutritional Values:

Carb:	3 Gr.
Proteins:	30 Gr.
Fats:	15 Gr.

Steps for Cooking:

1. First, put salt, Garam Masala, and pineapple juice in a bowl and mix everything with a fork.
2. Put the tuna fillet on a chopping board and divide it into four slices.
3. Transfer the tuna slice to a plate.
4. Spread the Garam Masala marinade on top and marinate for 15 minutes.
5. Heat the oil in a pan together with some onion pieces.
6. Add the ½ cup of almond milk and bring to a boil.
7. Boil for 5 minutes, then add the tuna marinated slices.
8. Coat the tuna with a lid and cook for 10 minutes.
9. When the almond Garam Masala tuna is cooked, turn it off and put it on two plates and serve.

Green Beans & Zucchini Chicken

Preapering	Servings	Cooking	Calories
20 Minutes	2 People	45 Minutes	310

Ingredients:

- 1 cup of chicken breast
- ½ cup of green beans
- 1 zucchini
- 1 tsp of ginger powder
- Olive oil to taste
- Salt and pepper to taste

Nutritional Values:

Carb:	8 Gr.
Proteins:	32 Gr.
Fats:	5 Gr.

Steps for Cooking:

1. Wash and trim, as the first operation, both the green beans and the zucchini, so divide them into small pieces.
2. Wash and dry chicken breast slices too.
3. Place the ginger powder, green beans and zucchini in the steamer basket along with the chicken slices.
4. Let the chicken and veggies steam for about half an hour.
5. Once cooked, serve the ginger chicken with the zucchini and green beans.

Mushroom & Tofu Stuffed Cod Fillet

Preapering	Servings	Cooking	Calories
5 Minutes	2 People	10 Minutes	320

Ingredients:

- 2 cups of cod fillet
- 3.5 oz of button mushrooms
- 1/3 cup of grated tofu cheese
- 1 garlic clove
- 1 teaspoon of chopped cilantro

Nutritional Values:

Carb:	3 Gr.
Proteins:	39Gr.
Fats:	14 Gr.

Steps for Cooking:

1. Wash and dry the cod fillet, remove the bones and then open it in two with a meat knife. Than remove any earthy parts of the button mushrooms, rinse them, dry and then chop finely.
2. Transfer all ingredients (carrots, shallots, lemon juice, oat milk, vegetable broth, salt, and pepper into a measuring cup).
3. Peel 1 garlic clove and then arrange it to brown in a pan with a drizzle of oil. Than Wash and chop the cilantro leaves as well.
4. Once golden and scented, remove the garlic and brown the chopped mushrooms for 5 minutes. Than Season with salt and pepper, add the cilantro too and turn off the heat.
5. Take the halved cod fillet and sprinkle it on both sides with salt and pepper.
6. Fill the inside of the cod with the grated tofu cheese and garlic mushrooms and then roll it up on itself. Seal it well helping with kitchen twine.
7. So, heat a bit of oil in a pan and brown the cod and garlic mushroom roll for 10/15 minutes, turning it on all sides.
8. Once cooked, remove the cod from the pan and let it rest for 5 minutes. Than, once cooked, remove the cod from the pan and let it rest for 5 minutes.
9. So, eliminate the kitchen string and cut the cod into rings.
10. Serve the stuffed cod sprinkled with the cilantro and garlic cooking juices.

Pecans & Cucumber-crusted Salmon

Preapering	Servings	Cooking	Calories
25 Minutes	2 People	12 Minutes	249

Ingredients:

- 14 oz of cleaned salmon fillet
- 2 tbsp of chopped pecans
- 1 tsp of chopped jalapeno
- 1 cucumber
- Olive oil to taste

Nutritional Values:

Carb:	6 Gr.
Proteins:	39 Gr.
Fats:	17 Gr.

Steps for Cooking:

1. As the first step for this salmon recipe, mince finely the pecans nuts.
2. Clean, rinse and brush the hake fillet with a bit of olive oil.
3. Peel and wash the cucumber and slice in a diagonally way.
4. Sprinkle the hake fillet with salt, pepper, chopped pecans and finally with the chopped jalapeno.
5. So, grasp a sheet of parchment paper and arrange it in a baking pan. Done this, put the hake fillet on the top of the sheet.
6. Coat completely the hake with sliced cucumber and season again with oil, salt, and pepper.
7. Place now the baking pan in the hot oven and bake at 338°F for 15 minutes about.
8. Passed this time, take away the salmon from the oven and slice it into many small slices.
9. Put the cucumber and pecans-covered salmon slices on two plates and serve.

Pepper & Tomato Salmon

Preapering	Servings	Cooking	Calories
15 Minutes	2 People	20 Minutes	290

Ingredients:

- 1 cup and 1/2 sliced salmon fillet
- 1 tsp of fenugreek seeds powder
- 1 chopped red bell pepper
- 12 cherry tomatoes
- ½ cup of fresh sugar free orange juice
- 1 tsp of chopped chives

Nutritional Values:

Carb:	10 Gr.
Proteins:	28 Gr.
Fats:	11 Gr.

Steps for Cooking:

1. First, wash, and remove the bones and skin from the salmon fillet, and split it into some slices.
2. Peel the red onion too, wash it and chop 1 tbsp. Than peel, remove the filaments and seeds and divide the red pepper into some slices too.
3. So, take a baking pan, add a little oil and then lay the slices of salmon on its top.
4. Drizzle with a bit of oil and sprinkle with the chopped red onion. Than wash the 12 cherry tomatoes too, drain and split them in half.
5. Spread the halved cherry tomatoes over the salmon slices and sprinkle with salt, fenugreek seeds powder, and pepper.
6. Finally, join the sliced pepper to the fish.
7. Place the salmon and peppers pan inside the oven preheated to 338 °F and cook for about 15 minutes.
8. After 8 minutes, turn the salmon, sprinkle it with the fresh orange juice and then cook for another 10 minutes.
9. Serve the salmon and veggies with a sprinkle of chopped chives still hot.

Pineapple & Soy Cheese Chicken Skewers

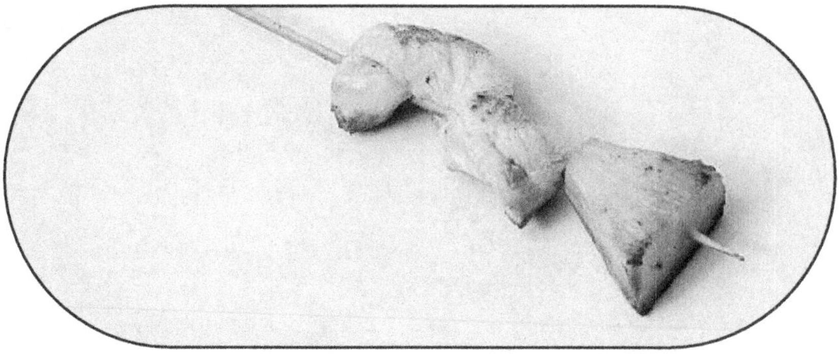

Preapering	Servings	Cooking	Calories
20 Minutes	2 People	20 Minutes	290

Ingredients:

- 14.1 oz of chicken breast
- 1/3 cup of fresh and sugar-free pineapple juice
- ½ cup of cubed soy cheese
- Salt and pepper to taste
- Olive oil to taste

Nutritional Values:

Carb:	3 Gr.
Proteins:	39 Gr.
Fats:	4 Gr.

Steps for Cooking:

1. So, start this anti-inflammatory dish by washing and drying the chicken breast, and splitting it into cubes.
2. Wash and dry the pineapple and extract 1/3 cup of its juice.
3. In the bowl with the just squeezed pineapple juice, add 3 tsp of olive oil, salt, pepper, and mix.
4. Now add the chicken cubes and stir everything well, so let marinate the meat for 30 minutes.
5. After 30 minutes, drain the chicken cubes from the marinade and skewer them on some skewers, alternating them with soy cheese cubes.
6. So, turn on a grill and, once hot enough, put the chicken and soy cheese on the grill.
7. Cook the skewers for 15/20 minutes, turning them every 5/6 minutes.
8. When the chicken is cooked, remove the soy cheese skewers from the grill, place them on serving dishes and serve.

Pistachio & Ginger Hake Fillet

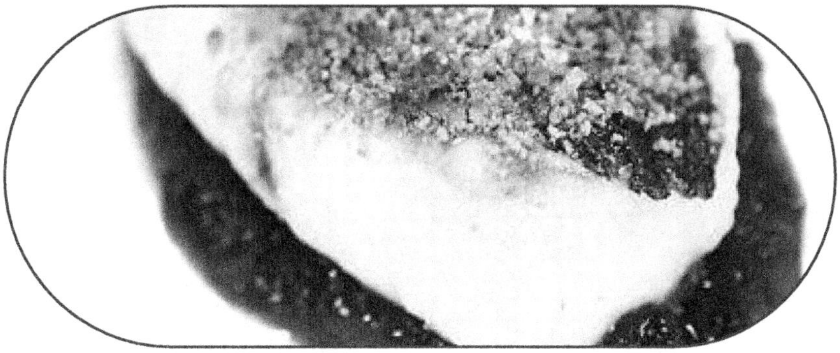

Preapering	Servings	Cooking	Calories
15 Minutes	2 People	20 Minutes	290

Ingredients:

- 10.5 oz of hake fillet
- 1.7 oz of toasted and chopped pistachios
- 1 tsp of fresh minced ginger
- 2 tbsp of low-fat white yogurt
- Olive oil to taste

Nutritional Values:

Carb:	6 Gr.
Proteins:	26 Gr.
Fats:	12 Gr.

Steps for Cooking:

1. Wash and dry the hake fillet, remove the excess bones, and then cut it into cubes.
2. Peel and wash a garlic clove and then chop it. Than put the pistachios in a non-stick pan and cook them for a couple of minutes.
3. So, heat 2 tsp of olive oil in another pan. Once hot, put the garlic clove to brown.
4. Add the hake fillet cubes and fresh minced ginger and mix.
5. Sauté the fish for 2 minutes and then add the yogurt.
6. Put together, sauté another 3 minutes and then add 3 tbsp of water.
7. Keep on cooking for another 9/10 minutes.
8. Flavor the hake with salt and pepper, add the chopped pistachios, stir well and then turn off.
9. Put the pistachio and ginger hake on serving plates, sprinkle with the cooking juices and serve this anti-inflammatory dish.

Radicchio & Roasted Turkey Eggs

Preapering	Servings	Cooking	Calories
10 Minutes	2 People	12 Minutes	210

Ingredients:

- 2 big size eggs
- ½ cup of chopped radicchio leaves
- 1/3 cup of roasted turkey
- 1 tsp of cumin powder
- 1 tbsp of olive oil

Nutritional Values:

Carb:	4 Gr.
Proteins:	25 Gr.
Fats:	10 Gr.

Steps for Cooking:

1. As the first thing to do for this recipe, wash and dry the radicchio leaves, then chop them very finely.
2. So, grasp a non-stick pan to heat with the olive oil.
3. Once it will be quite hot, add the chopped radicchio and brown it for 5 minutes, flavoring it with a pinch of salt and pepper, and cook for another 2 minutes.
4. In a dish or bowl, batter the 2 eggs with cumin powder and after this 2 further cooking minutes pour the eggs into the pan with the radicchio.
5. Add the thinly sliced roasted turkey and stir constantly. Form many separate pieces for the eggs.
6. So, proceed on cooking for five minutes and then transfer the radicchio and turkey eggs to a serving dish, so serve.

Sage & Beet Greens Chipotle Crusted Cod

Preapering	Servings	Cooking	Calories
20 Minutes	2 People	10 Minutes	250

Ingredients:

- 10.5 oz of cod fillet
- ¼ cup of cooked beets green
- 1 tbsp fresh sage leaves
- 2 tbsp of spiced panko
- 1 tsp of chopped chipotle

Nutritional Values:

Carb:	3 Gr.
Proteins:	29 Gr.
Fats:	8 Gr.

Steps for Cooking:

1. Pour the spiced panko, as first operation, into a bowl together with the chopped chipotle, sage leaves salt, pepper and some olive oil.
2. Chop the cooked beets green finely and put them in the bowl with the marjoram and chipotle panko.
3. Combine all the ingredients so you will ha your cod breading.
4. Take the already cleaned and no bone cod fillets and coat them entirely with the beets green and chipotle breading.
5. So, now let heat a pan with oil and cook the cod fillet for 5 minutes on each side.
6. Once cooked, switch off the heat and cut the cod into some slices.
7. Put the cod slices on 2 plates and serve this anti-inflammatory dish.

Salmon Spinach & Peach Poke Bowl

Preapering	Servings	Cooking	Calories
10 Minutes	2 People	5 Minutes	235

Ingredients:

- 3.5 oz of cubed peach
- 1/3 cup of smoked salmon
- ¼ cup of chopped spinach leaves
- 2 tsp of chopped cashews
- Lemon juice to taste

Nutritional Values:

Carb:	11 Gr.
Proteins:	25 Gr.
Fats:	12 Gr.

Steps for Cooking:

1. Start to prepare this anti-inflammatory salad bowl by peeling and cubing the peach.
2. Meanwhile, boil the fresh spinach leaves for 5 minutes in boiling salt water and drain.
3. So, put the spinach in a bowl and then put the peach cubes and chopped smoked salmon next to it.
4. Season with olive oil, lemon juice, salt and pepper, sprinkle with chopped cashew and serve in this salad bowl.

Soy Cheese & Jalapeno Turkey Meatloaf

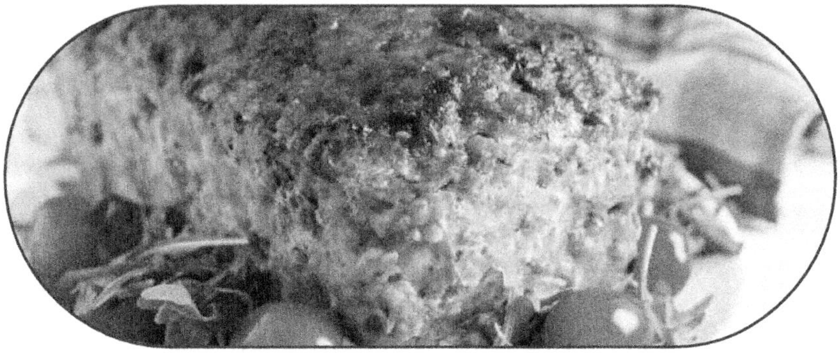

Preapering	Servings	Cooking	Calories
5 Minutes	2 People	15 Minutes	410

Ingredients:

- 1 cup and ½ of ground turkey lean breast
- 3 tbsp of almond flour
- 1 cup of soy cheese
- 1 tsp of smoked paprika
- 1 egg
- 1 chopped jalapeno

Nutritional Values:

Carb:	4 Gr.
Proteins:	48 Gr.
Fats:	22 Gr.

Steps for Cooking:

1. First, cut, in a bowl, pour the minced turkey with the egg, soy cheese, almond flour, smoked paprika, a pinch of salt, a pinch of pepper and the chopped jalapeno.
2. So, start working on these ingredients until you will obtain a homogeneous mixture.
3. Then roll out the jalapeno turkey dough on a sheet of baking paper to create a sort of rectangle.
4. Through a piece of paper, roll up the meatloaf and tie its ends with the help of kitchen twine.
5. So, transfer the jalapeno soy cheese and turkey meatloaf into a pan, add a bit of vegetable broth and transfer to the oven.
6. Cook at 392° F for about 20 minutes about.
7. Check the cooking and, once well cooked, take away the jalapeno turkey meatloaf from the oven.
8. Let it rest for a couple of minutes, then split the turkey and soy cheese meatloaf into slices, arrange the slices on serving plates and serve.

Squash & Zucchini Orange Turkey

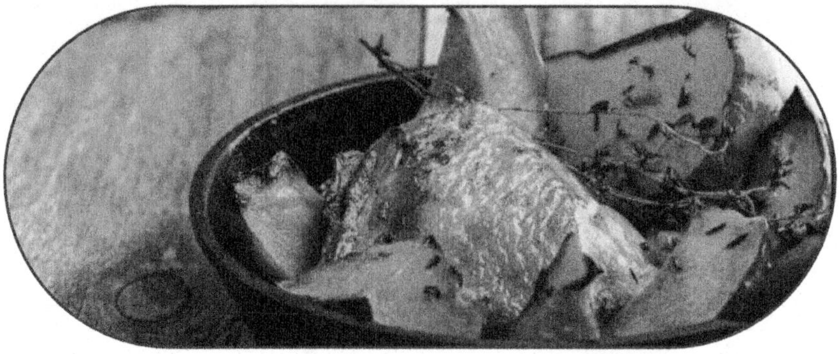

Preapering	Servings	Cooking	Calories
45 Minutes	2 People	30 Minutes	390

Ingredients:

- 08. lbs of turkey breast
- 7 oz of squash pulp
- 3 tbsp of chopped zucchini
- 1 tsp of amchoor powder
- ½ orange

Nutritional Values:

Carb:	15 Gr.
Proteins:	55 Gr.
Fats:	10 Gr.

Steps for Cooking:

1. As first step, arrange the already cleaned turkey breasts in a bowl, adding the orange juice, amchoor powder, salt, pepper, and oil and let marinate for at least 15 minutes.
2. Meanwhile, eliminate the peel and seeds from the squash and divide its pulp into slices.
3. Peel, rinse and chop the 3 tbsp of zucchini too.
4. Brush a baking pan with olive oil and put the sliced squash inside.
5. So, flavor the squash with oil, salt and pepper and place in the oven to cook at 375°F for 15 minutes.
6. After 15 minutes, take the amchoor squash baking pan out of the oven and add the sliced turkey and chopped zucchini.
7. Put again back this pan in the oven and cook for another 20 minutes.
8. After cooking, take the turkey, zucchini and squash baking pan out of the oven. Put these anti-inflammatory ingredients in two serving plates and serve.

Tuna & Egg-stuffed Zucchini

Preapering	Servings	Cooking	Calories
15 Minutes	2 People	12 Minutes	290

Ingredients:

- 2 zucchinis
- 2 eggs
- ¼ cup of drained tuna in oil
- ½ scallion
- 1 lemon

Nutritional Values:

Carb:	7 Gr.
Proteins:	22 Gr.
Fats:	14 Gr.

Steps for Cooking:

1. First step: wash and dry the 2 zucchinis, halve, remove the stone and remove some of its pulp with the help of a spoon.
2. Sprinkle the halved zucchini with lemon juice.
3. So, place the lemon-halved zucchini s in a baking pan and add oil, salt, and pepper.
4. Now, you should pour the broken eggs into the center of the zucchini and sprinkle with the diced drained and chopped tuna in oil.
5. Put the baking pan in the oven and cook at 392°F for 12/15 minutes.
6. Once perfectly cooked, take the baking pan out of the oven, put the filled zucchinis with eggs and tuna on the plates and serve.

White Zucchini & Chicken Spicy Soup

Preapering	Servings	Cooking	Calories
15 Minutes	2 People	20 Minutes	210

Ingredients:

- 2 white zucchinis
- 1 cup of cleaned and cubed chicken breast
- 2 tsp of freshly chopped cilantro leaves
- 1 tbsp of Garam Masala
- 1 tsp of chopped bay leaves

Nutritional Values:

Carb:	7 Gr.
Proteins:	26 Gr.
Fats:	12 Gr.

Steps for Cooking:

1. Peel and wash the 2 white zucchinis, rinse them under cold water and then cut them into cubes.
2. Wash and dry the bay and cilantro leaves. Than pour 3 tsp of oil into the pan.
3. When it will be hot, brown 1 garlic clove and the fresh chopped herbs.
4. Now add the white zucchinis cube and sauté for 10 minutes then, remove the garlic clove.
5. Cook for another 4 minutes, add salt and pepper and Garam Masala powder. Add 1 cup of water too and keep on cooking for another 5 minutes.
6. Now, rinse the cleaned chicken breast and cube it.
7. Now arrange the cubed meat in the pan with bay, cilantro and white zucchini.
8. Cook for another 15 minutes.
9. Turn off, put the spicy chicken and white zucchini soup on serving plates and serve.
10. Now pour the contents of the pan into the pan with the sliced Alaska Pollock fillet.

Avocado & Jalapeno Snack Salad

Preapering	Servings	Cooking	Calories
20 Minutes	2 People	6 Minutes	290

Ingredients:

- 1 avocado
- 2 tsp of cashews
- ½ cup of tofu cheese
- 1 ripe tomato
- 1 lemon
- 1 scallion

Nutritional Values:

Carb:	5 Gr.
Proteins:	23 Gr.
Fats:	16 Gr.

Steps for Cooking:

1. As the first step, peel the scallion, wash it and chop it.
2. Rinse the tofu cheese and then cut it into some pieces.
3. Put some olive oil in a pan, and let it heat. Once it will be quite hot, put the scallion to brown.
4. Now add the tofu cheese and sauté for two minutes. Peel the avocado, wash, pit and halve.
5. So, divide its pulp into cubes and then arrange the cubes in a bowl.
6. Season the avocado cubes with a bit of lime juice.
7. Wash the ripe tomato and then divide it into cubes. Join the tomato cubes with the avocado ones.
8. Add the sautéed tofu cheese and cashews to the bowl too.
9. At this point, you can season your anti-inflammatory snack salad with apple cider vinegar, salt and pepper, and a tbsp of olive oil and serve.

Banana & Cherries Fruits Bowl

Preapering	Servings	Cooking	Calories
10 Minutes	2 People	0 Minutes	160

Ingredients:

- ½ bananas
- 6 cherries
- 1 cup of low fat white yogurt
- 1 tbsp chia seeds

Nutritional Values:

Carb:	15 Gr.
Proteins:	8 Gr.
Fats:	1 Gr.

Steps for Cooking:

1. As the first step, peel, wash and slice the half banana.
2. Wash and pit the cherries then cut them into pieces.
3. Put banana slices and cherry pieces in the glass of the blender, along with the low-fat yogurt.
4. So, work on these fruits and yogurt until you get a thick and creamy mixture.
5. Once done, pour the mixture into two bowls.
6. Sprinkle with the chia seeds and serve your snack.

Chipotle & Cilantro Scrambled Eggs

Preapering	Servings	Cooking	Calories
10 Minutes	2 People	5 Minutes	180

Ingredients:

- 3 eggs
- 1 tsp chopped cilantro leaves
- 1 tsp chopped chipotle
- 1 tsp chopped rosemary
- 1 tsp chopped fresh mint

Nutritional Values:

Carb:	1 Gr.
Proteins:	15 Gr.
Fats:	12 Gr.

Steps for Cooking:

1. As the first step, shell the three eggs directly in a bowl and add salt, cilantro, chopped chipotle, rosemary and mint leaves.
2. So, batter the eggs with a fork until you get a homogeneous mixture.
3. Now, you can just heat a drizzle of oil in a pan and, once hot, pour the chipotle egg mixture.
4. Cook the eggs for 5-6 minutes, stirring often.
5. Once the scrambled eggs are done, turn them off, split them into two plates and serve.

Flaxseeds Mango & Apricot Bowl

Preapering	Servings	Cooking	Calories
10 Minutes	2 People	2 Minutes	170

Ingredients:

- 1 mango
- 2 apricots
- ½ cup of low fat yogurt
- 1 tbsp of flax seeds

Nutritional Values:

Carb:	15 Gr.
Proteins:	10 Gr.
Fats:	2 Gr.

Steps for Cooking:

1. As first step, peel both mango and apricots, remove their central stone and cut them into pieces.
2. Put the mango and apricot pieces inside the glass of the blender. Add the low-fat yogurt too.
3. Blend until you will see a truly thick and creamy mixture.
4. So, pour this just obtained mixture into two bowls.
5. Decorate with the flax seeds and serve.

Medlar & Strawberry Yogurt Cup

Preapering	Servings	Cooking	Calories
20 Minutes	2 People	0 Minutes	220

Ingredients:

- 2 cups of low-fat white yogurt
- 8 pitted medlars
- ¼ cup of sugar free soy milk
- 2 tbsp of honey
- 2 tbsp of chopped strawberries

Nutritional Values:

Carb:	24 Gr.
Proteins:	7 Gr.
Fats:	8 Gr.

Steps for Cooking:

1. As first step for the recipe, pour the 2 cups of yogurt, honey, and sugar free coconut milk into a bowl.
2. So, you should take an immersion blender and use it to mince all these ingredients, until smooth.
3. Arrange the just obtained mixture in a low side container.
4. So, close this container and place it in the freezer.
5. Let the mixture rest in the freezer for about 3 hours, taking care to mix it every 20/25 minutes.
6. After this time indicated, take out the yogurt mixture from the fridge, divide it into pieces and pour it into the blender.
7. Blend again for 40 seconds, then turn off the blender and distribute the frozen yogurt into two bowls.
8. Add the pitted Medlar, sprinkle with chopped strawberries and serve.

Rosemary Almonds & Soy Cheese Canapés

Preapering	Servings	Cooking	Calories
20 Minutes	2 People	10 Minutes	300

Ingredients:

- 4 little slices of whole wheat bread (1 cup total)
- 3.5 oz of soy cheese
- 1 tbsp of chopped rosemary
- 1 orange juice and peel
- 2 tbsp of chopped almonds

Nutritional Values:

Carb:	29 Gr.
Proteins:	11 Gr.
Fats:	6 Gr.

Steps for Cooking:

1. Start this snack recipe by washing and chopping 1 tbsp of rosemary.
2. Dab and cube the soy cheese and put it directly in a mixer.
3. Blend the soy cheese after adding the chopped rosemary, the juice and the orange peel too.
4. Join a pinch of salt and pepper too to the soy cheese cream.
5. Once you have obtained a thick mixture, spread it to your canapés.
6. Decorate with orange peel and chopped almonds and serve.

Strawberry & Pineapple Ginger Popsicles

Preapering	Servings	Cooking	Calories
10 Minutes	2 People	0 Minutes	35

Ingredients:

- 4 tbsp of almond milk
- 2 tbsp of fresh sugar free pineapple juice
- 8 strawberries
- 1 tsp of powdered ginger
- 2 tsp of honey

Nutritional Values:

Carb:	2 Gr.
Proteins:	1 Gr.
Fats:	2 Gr.

Steps for Cooking:

1. Start with washing and let drying the eight strawberries, the chop.
2. Pour now the fresh pineapple juice into the glass of a blender.
3. Also add the almond milk, ginger powder, honey and chopped strawberries.
4. Work these ingredients and mince everything at maximum speed until you will have a smooth mixture.
5. So, now grasp the popsicle molds and transfer the strawberry and ginger mixture inside.
6. So, let rest in the freezer for at least 3 hours and a half.
7. Once this time is passed, you can take the strawberry pineapple and ginger popsicles and serve them.

Zucchini & Soy Cheese Jalapeno Nuggets

Preapering	Servings	Cooking	Calories
10 Minutes	2 People	15 Minutes	100

Ingredients:

- 1 halved long zucchini
- 4 pieces of soy cheese
- 1 tsp of chopped jalapeno
- 2 tsp of olive oil

Nutritional Values:

Carb:	14 Gr.
Proteins:	9 Gr.
Fats:	3 Gr.

Steps for Cooking:

1. As the first step for this recipe, preheat the oven to 392° F.
2. Peel the zucchini, wash, halve horizontally and lightly scoop their pulp.
3. Place a piece of soy cheese in each zucchini halve.
4. Sprinkle both halves with chopped jalapeno and arrange the zucchini in a baking pan.
5. Cook the filled zucchini halves for 15 minutes about.
6. Once completely cooked, serve this soy cheese and jalapeno filled zucchinis still hot as a snack.

Apple & Mushroom Stuffed Chipotle Lettuce

Preapering	Servings	Cooking	Calories
15 Minutes	2 People	0 Minutes	190

Ingredients:

- 5 large lettuce leaves
- 6 button mushrooms
- 1 cubed apple
- 2 tsp of low-fat white yogurt
- 2 tsp of apple cider vinegar
- 1 tsp of chopped chipotle

Nutritional Values:

Carb:	5 Gr.
Proteins:	24Gr.
Fats:	4 Gr.

Steps for Cooking:

1. Start the recipe by peeling, washing and drying the apple, then halve, remove the seeds, then divide it and into some small cubes.
2. Wash the lettuce leaves and dry them as well. Finely chop 1 of these lettuce leaves and place the other 4 leaves aside.
3. Wash and dry the six-button mushrooms and then divide them into small slices.
4. Now put the apple, chopped leaves and sliced mushroom in a bowl.
5. Join the apple cider vinegar and stir everything. Add the white yogurt, the chopped chipotle, a pinch of salt and pepper and stir all the ingredients.
6. Now grasp the whole lettuce leaves and start to stuff them with the apple and mushroom filling. Placing the stuffed lettuce in the serving dish and serve.

Baked Soy Cheese Artichokes

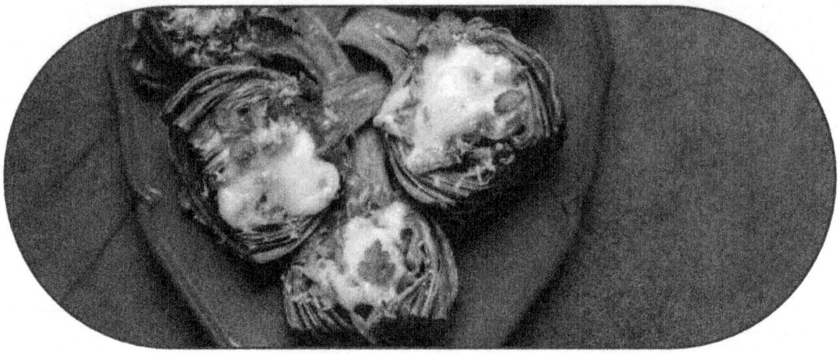

Preapering	Servings	Cooking	Calories
15 Minutes	2 People	20 Minutes	126

Ingredients:

- 2 artichokes
- 1/2 cup of soy cheese
- A lemon
- 1 chopped jalapeno
- Salt and pepper to taste
- Olive oil to taste

Nutritional Values:

Carb:	10 Gr.
Proteins:	4 Gr.
Fats:	5 Gr.

Steps for Cooking:

1. So, the first step for this anti-inflammatory recipe is cleaning the artichokes. So, eliminate the stem and outer hardest leaves.
2. Halve the artichokes so split them into wedges and arrange them to wash in a bowl with water and lemon juice.
3. Chop the jalapeno and dab the soy cheese.
4. So, brush a pan with oil and then arrange the soy cheese and artichokes.
5. Sprinkle everything with chopped jalapeno oil, salt and pepper and then bake at 392°F for 20/22 minutes.
6. Once cooked, serve the soy cheese and jalapeno artichokes directly on two serving plates.

Broccoli Fenugreek Seeds & Ginger Tofu

Preapering	Servings	Cooking	Calories
15 Minutes	2 People	10 Minutes	190

Ingredients:

- 14 oz of tofu cheese
- ½ cup of broccoli
- 1 tsp of fresh minced ginger
- 1 tsp of chopped chives
- 1 tsp of fenugreek seeds
- ½ lemon juice

Nutritional Values:

Carb:	5 Gr.
Proteins:	25 Gr.
Fats:	4 Gr.

Steps for Cooking:

1. As first step for this recipe, wash and dry the half cup of broccoli florets, so divide them into many pieces. Wash and chop the chives as well.
2. Rinse and cube the tofu cheese.
3. So, combine together in a bowl, the olive oil, lemon juice, salt, minced ginger and fenugreek seeds with a fork. Mix until you have a perfect emulsion.
4. So, take now one sheet of aluminum foil and place the tofu inside of it. Add the minced broccoli tops and then pour over the lemon, fenugreek seeds and ginger emulsion.
5. Seal well the tofu foil.
6. Put the just prepare foil directly in the oven and cook at 338°F for 10 minutes.
7. Once ready, serve the tofu with the broccoli and sprinkled with the spicy emulsion.

Chia Seeds & Spinach Avocado Rolls

Preapering	Servings	Cooking	Calories
10 Minutes	2 People	10 Minutes	280

Ingredients:

- 8 avocado long slices
- ½ cup of cooked spinach
- ¼ tsp of nutmeg
- 1 tsp of chia seeds

Nutritional Values:

Carb:	8 Gr.
Proteins:	18 Gr.
Fats:	18 Gr.

Steps for Cooking:

1. First, take a bowl and pour the rinsed spinach inside.
2. Flavor it with a spoonful of olive oil, nutmeg, salt and pepper.
3. Add the chia seeds to the spinach. Stir everything with a fork to flavor.
4. Now grasp the avocado slices and fill them with the spinach and chia seeds mixture.
5. Close the rolls with a toothpick and arrange them in the fridge to rest for 1 hour before serving.

Cucumber & Pineapple Tofu Skewers

Preapering	Servings	Cooking	Calories
20 Minutes	2 People	10 Minutes	170

Ingredients:

- 14 oz of cubed tofu cheese
- 2 limes
- 1 cup of cubed pineapple pulp
- 1 cup of cubed cucumber
- 1 tbsp of orange juice
- Olive oil to taste

Nutritional Values:

Carb:	18 Gr.
Proteins:	22 Gr.
Fats:	3 Gr.

Steps for Cooking:

1. As the first operation for this skewer recipe, rinse and cut the tofu into some cubes.
2. Arrange now, these vegan cubes in a bowl. Than join the salt, and pepper and sprinkle with the filtered orange juice.
3. Cover the bowl and put the orange tofu to marinate in the fridge for at least 10 minutes.
4. Passed this time, take the tofu cubes back, and start to create these anti-inflammatory vegan skewers.
5. Put the orange tofu cubes on the aluminum skewers.
6. Add pineapple and cucumber cubes, so start to alternate ingredients until they will be ended.
7. Now, it's time to heat a grill and, once very hot, put the tofu and veggies skewers to the grill.
8. Cook for 2 minutes on each side and then take out off the grill.
9. Put the tofu and veggies skewers on serving plates, sprinkle with a little orange marinating liquid and serve this vegan dish.

Green Beans Turnips & Soy Cheese Cream

Preapering	Servings	Cooking	Calories
15 Minutes	2 People	20 Minutes	180

Ingredients:

- 1 cup of soy cheese
- 1/3 cup of turnips
- 3.5 oz of green beans
- 2 tsp of fresh sugar-free orange juice
- 1 tsp turmeric powder

Nutritional Values:

Carb:	13 Gr.
Proteins:	15 Gr.
Fats:	8 Gr.

Steps for Cooking:

1. Start this recipe, by rinsing the soy cheese, cutting it into cubes and putting it in a bowl.
2. Add the orange juice and turmeric powder and let it marinate for 10 minutes.
3. So, now you can trim the green beans, wash them and then divide them into 3 pieces.
4. Peel and wash the turnips and then cut them into slices.
5. Passed 10 minutes, heat a spoonful of olive oil in a pan and, once hot enough, put the turnips and green beans to cook for 15 minutes.
6. Now add the cubed soy cheese with the orange and turmeric marinating liquid, season with salt and pepper and keep on cooking for another 5 minutes, turning everything often.
7. After this time, turn off the heat and put the soy cheese, turnips and green beans on serving plates.
8. Sprinkle with the orange turmeric juice cooking liquid and serve.

Orange & Marjoram Veggies

Preapering	Servings	Cooking	Calories
20 Minutes	2 People	10 Minutes	480

Ingredients:

- 1 avocado
- 4 cherry tomatoes
- 2 leeks
- ½ cup of orange juice
- 1 tbsp of chopped marjoram
- 1 tsp of turmeric powder

Nutritional Values:

Carb:	7 Gr.
Proteins:	50 Gr.
Fats:	18 Gr.

Steps for Cooking:

1. So, start this anti-inflammatory recipe by cleaning the avocado: peel it, eliminate the stone, wash it under running water and then dry it. So, cut the pulp into thin strip.
2. Wash the four cherry tomatoes too, dry them and then halve.
3. Clean the leeks then slice. Than, in a small bowl, now put together the orange juice, turmeric powder, olive oil and the tbsp of chopped marjoram. Add a pinch of salt and pepper too. Stir well to mix everything.
4. So, take a pan large enough.
5. Place the avocado strips on the bottom. Sprinkle them with a pinch of salt.
6. Now place the leek on top of the avocado slices.
7. Place the cherry tomatoes and then sprinkle everything with the orange and marjoram marinade.
8. Now, place the veggies orange pan to bake in a preheated oven at 392 °F for 10 minutes.
9. Serve the orange veggies when they will be cooled.

Peach & Veggies Salad

Preapering	Servings	Cooking	Calories
15 Minutes	2 People	0 Minutes	370

Ingredients:

- 10 oz of sliced peach
- ½ avocado
- 1 carrot
- 2 tsp soy sauce
- 2 tsp of Garam Masala
- 1 tbsp of rice vinegar

Nutritional Values:

Carb:	32 Gr.
Proteins:	8 Gr.
Fats:	12 Gr.

Steps for Cooking:

1. Start this recipe by preparing the dressing marinade.
2. In a small bowl, pour a bit of olive oil, rice vinegar soy sauce, and Garam Masala powder.
3. Now take the sliced peach and join to the other ingredients.
4. Cover the peach and Garam Masala marinade with a cling film and arrange in the fridge to flavor for fifteen minutes.
5. So, start to clean the veggies: halve the avocado lengthwise, remove the peel and the central core and then divide it into cubes.
6. Peel and wash the carrot too, halve and through a peeler split it into thin strips.
7. Now take a bowl and put the Garam Masala peaches in.
8. Join the carrot strips and avocado.
9. So, pour over a little olive oil and a sprinkle of salt and pepper and serve.

Radicchio & Pear Soy Cheese Salad

Preapering	Servings	Cooking	Calories
15 Minutes	2 People	0 Minutes	150

Ingredients:

- ½ cup of radicchio leaves
- 7 oz of soy cheese
- 1 pear
- 2 bay leaves
- Apple cider vinegar to taste
- Olive oil to taste

Nutritional Values:

Carb:	11 Gr.
Proteins:	18 Gr.
Fats:	3 Gr.

Steps for Cooking:

1. As the first operation for this recipe, dab and cube the tofu cheese.
2. Wash both the bay leaves.
3. Meanwhile, halve the pear, eliminate the seeds, and split it into cubes.
4. Wash and dry the radicchio leaves, so cut them into thin slices.
5. Arrange the tofu cubes in a bowl.
6. Add radicchio leaves, chopped sage and pear to the same salad bowl.
7. Season the salad with oil, salt, pepper, and apple cider vinegar, stir to flavor and serve this vegan salad.

Sweet & Sour Zucchini & Asparagus

Preapering	Servings	Cooking	Calories
10 Minutes	2 People	25 Minutes	70

Ingredients:

- 14 oz of sliced zucchini
- 10.5 oz of fresh asparagus
- 1 lime
- 3 tbsp of apple cider vinegar
- 1 tsp of ginger powder

Nutritional Values:

Carb:	7 Gr.
Proteins:	6 Gr.
Fats:	3 Gr.

Steps for Cooking:

1. The first step for this recipe, grasp a fairly large bowl and put the vinegar, 1 tsp of olive oil, ginger powder, salt and pepper and the filtered lime juice inside. So, stir and combine well.
2. Now, peel, wash and slice one cup of zucchini. Take these slices and place them in the bowl with the marinade. Let the zucchini marinate for 30 minutes at room temperature.
3. Now, you can trim the asparagus, wash and dry it.
4. Boil a pot full of water and salt then cook the asparagus for 10 minutes.
5. After 10 minutes, drain and let the asparagus cool.
6. So, now you can place a pan in the heat with some oil. Once the oil will be hot, add the zucchini slices with all the lime ginger marinade liquid.
7. Cook for 5 minutes and then add the asparagus. Stir, season with salt and cook for another 5 minutes.
8. Once the veggies are done place them on serving plates with the cooking liquid and serve.

Tofu & Cashews Cucumber Rolls

Preapering	Servings	Cooking	Calories
10 Minutes	2 People	10 Minutes	130

Ingredients:

- 4 cucumber slices
- ½ cup of tofu cheese
- 1 tsp of ginger powder
- 1 tbsp of chopped cashews and nuts
- ¼ cup of kale leaves

Nutritional Values:

Carb:	5 Gr.
Proteins:	10 Gr.
Fats:	8 Gr.

Steps for Cooking:

1. First, take a bowl and pour the rinsed tofu cheese inside.
2. Flavor it with a spoonful of olive oil, ginger powder, salt and pepper.
3. Wash and chop finely the kale leaves
4. Finely chop the cashew nuts and then add them to the ginger tofu cheese. Stir everything with a fork to flavor.
5. Now grasp the cucumber slices and fill them with the tofu cashew mixture and add a little chopped kale leaves to each slice.
6. Close the tofu cucumber rolls with a toothpick and arrange them in the fridge to rest for 1 hour before serving.

Walnuts Leeks & Kale Salad

Preapering	Servings	Cooking	Calories
15 Minutes	2 People	15 Minutes	100

Ingredients:

- 1 leek sliced
- 1 cup of kale leaves
- 1 tsp of chopped rosemary
- 4 tbsp of finely chopped walnuts
- Olive oil to taste

Nutritional Values:

Carb:	8 Gr.
Proteins:	7 Gr.
Fats:	9 Gr.

Steps for Cooking:

1. First, clean wash and dry the leek, so slice it.
2. Season the leek slices with salt and pepper.
3. Wash and dry the rosemary and then chop it.
4. Put the finely chopped walnuts on a plate and flour the leek slices on both sides.
5. Heat a tablespoon of oil in a pan and cook the walnuts breaded leeks for 10 minutes, turning it once.
6. Once they are cooked, take the leek walnut slices away from the pan and let them cool onto a plate.
7. At the same time, wash the kale leaves and chop them.
8. Season all these veggies with oil, salt and apple cider vinegar.
9. Now put the leek slice slices on serving plates, surround them with the kale salad and serve.

Watermelon & Coriander Tofu Cubes

Preapering	Servings	Cooking	Calories
10 Minutes	2 People	15 Minutes	410

Ingredients:

- 14 oz of cubed tofu cheese
- ¼ of watermelon
- 1 tsp of chopped coriander
- the zest of a lemon
- 2 tsp of chopped hazelnuts

Nutritional Values:

Carb:	12 Gr.
Proteins:	48 Gr.
Fats:	7 Gr.

Steps for Cooking:

1. First, grasp the tofu cubes and arrange them in a salad bowl sprinkle with a little salt.
2. Wash the coriander leaves.
3. In the meantime, peel the ¼ of the watermelon, take the pulp and then split it into cubes too.
4. So, arrange the watermelon cubes in the mixer glass, add a little oil, salt and pepper and mince it to form a sauce.
5. Put the just-created watermelon sauce on the bottom of the plates, spread over the tofu cubes, and the chopped coriander and serve.

Zucchini Jalapeno Coleslaw

Preapering	Servings	Cooking	Calories
20 Minutes	2 People	10 Minutes	60

Ingredients:

- 1 cup of cabbage leaves
- 1 tsp of cumin powder
- 4 zucchini slices
- 2 tsp of pink peppercorns
- Apple cider vinegar to taste

Nutritional Values:

Carb:	8 Gr.
Proteins:	5 Gr.
Fats:	2 Gr.

Steps for Cooking:

1. The first step for this recipe: wash and dry the cabbage leaves, chop and season with salt, cumin powder and pepper.
2. Arrange the cumin cabbage in a pan with olive oil and cook in the oven at 392°F for 15 minutes.
3. Meanwhile, peel the zucchini and split them into thin slices.
4. Once the cabbage is cooked, take it away from the oven and let it rest for 10 minutes.
5. Divide the sliced zucchini between two serving plates.
6. Place the cabbage on top of the zucchini slices.
7. Pour a bit of oil, two apple cider vinegar, pink peppercorns, salt and pepper in a bowl and mix.
8. So, sprinkle the coleslaw with the pink pepper emulsion and serve.

Zucchini Mango & Grapefruit Salad

Preapering	Servings	Cooking	Calories
10Minutes	2 People	0 Minutes	170

Ingredients:

- 1 cup and ½ of zucchini slices
- ½ grapefruit
- 3 cabbage leaves
- ½ lime
- ½ mango

Nutritional Values:

Carb:	25 Gr.
Proteins:	6 Gr.
Fats:	2 Gr.

Steps for Cooking:

1. As the first operation for this recipe, peel and rinse them under cold water the grapefruit, then slice it into wedges.
2. Peel the mango too, remove its stone, and then divide it into cubes.
3. Arrange both the mango and grapefruit in a bowl.
4. Add the sliced zucchini. So, add a bit of oil, salt, pepper, and filtered half-lime juice.
5. So, stir all the anti-inflammatory salad ingredients and serve this anti-inflammatory salad.

Apple & Peach Cashew Milkshake

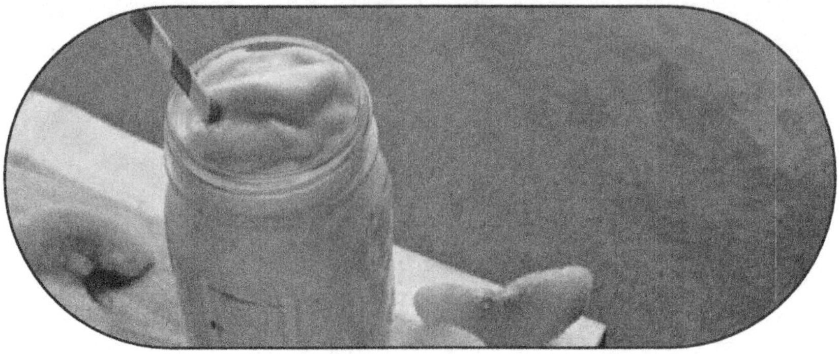

Preapering	Servings	Cooking	Calories
15 Minutes	2 People	0 Minutes	120

Ingredients:

- 1 apple
- 1 peach
- 1 cup of sugar free soy milk
- 2 tsp of chopped cashews and nuts

Nutritional Values:

Carb:	15 Gr.
Proteins:	5 Gr.
Fats:	4 Gr.

Steps for Cooking:

1. So, start this recipe by peeling both the peach and apple, removing the seeds and stone, washing it, and cutting it into pieces.
2. Pour the apple and peach pieces into the blender glass and mince them for 45 seconds about.
3. Now add the sugar-free milk and blend for another 25 seconds.
4. Now add the ice cubes (the quantity you like more) and mince until you will have a true thick smoothie.
5. Transfer the peach and apple smoothie into the glasses, add the straws too inside, sprinkle with chopped cashews and serve.

Apricot & Hazelnuts Coconut

Preapering	Servings	Cooking	Calories
10 Minutes	2 People	0 Minutes	200

Ingredients:

- 1 cup of sugar free coconut milk
- 4 pitted apricots
- 2 tsp of chopped hazelnuts
- 4 tsp of coconut flour
- ½ teaspoon of vanilla extract
- 1 pinch of nutmeg

Nutritional Values:

Carb:	6 Gr.
Proteins:	12Gr.
Fats:	9 Gr.

Steps for Cooking:

1. As the first operation for this dessert cream, combine the coconut milk, hazelnuts, coconut flour, nutmeg and vanilla extract in a bowl.
2. Whisk these anti-inflammatory ingredients until the mixture has thickened enough.
3. Let it rest for 20 minutes in the fridge.
4. After this time indicated, remove your creams from the fridge.
5. Meanwhile, wash and dry the apricots, pit and slice.
6. Serve your cream accompanied by the just sliced apricots.

Avocado Kiwi & Banana Smoothie

Preapering	Servings	Cooking	Calories
15 Minutes	2 People	0 Minutes	390

Ingredients:

- 2 bananas
- 2 little size avocados
- 2 kiwis
- 1 cup of low-fat white yogurt
- 1 glass of sugar free coconut milk

Nutritional Values:

Carb:	35 Gr.
Proteins:	11 Gr.
Fats:	18 Gr.

Steps for Cooking:

1. As the first step for this recipe, peel the avocados, remove the central core, and split them into small pieces.
2. Do the same with the kiwis but divide them into 4 parts.
3. So, wash both bananas, peel them, and cut them into cubes.
4. Put the banana cubes, kiwi parts, and avocado pieces in the blender.
5. Add the low-fat yoghurt and coconut milk and mince everything for 70 seconds, to have a creamy and thick smoothie.
6. So, distribute the anti-inflammatory smoothie between two glasses and serve.

Banana Pistachio Chips

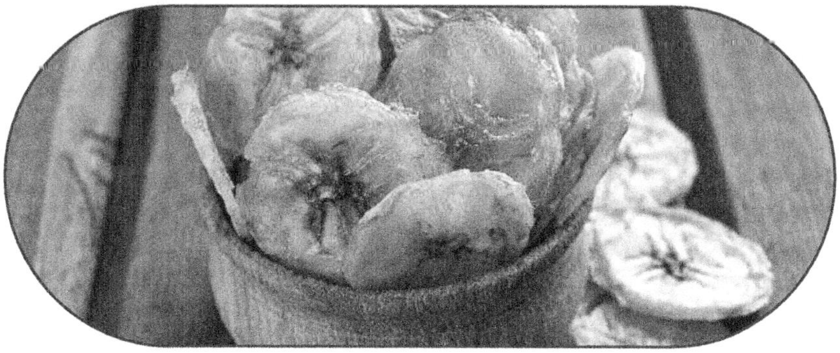

Preapering	Servings	Cooking	Calories
10 Minutes	2 People	20 Minutes	140

Ingredients:

- ½ banana
- 2 tbsp of chopped pistachios
- 1 tbsp of soy flour
- 1 tbsp of almond flour
- ¼ cup water

Nutritional Values:

Carb:	28 Gr.
Proteins:	4 Gr.
Fats:	6 Gr.

Steps for Cooking:

1. The first operation for this fruit chips recipe: peel, and slice the banana.
2. Now, in a bowl, dissolve the almond flour and soy one with the water, mixing well.
3. Season with salt and pepper. In a second bowl pour the chopped pistachios instead.
4. So, bread the banana slices first in the almond and soy flour batter, then in the pistachios and arrange them on a baking sheet lined with parchment paper.
5. When all the banana pistachio chips have been well-breaded, bake in the oven at 356° C for 10 minutes about
6. Once ready, serve these breaded banana and pistachios chips hot.

Banana & Avocado Almond Yogurt

Preapering	Servings	Cooking	Calories
10 Minutes	2 People	0 Minutes	290

Ingredients:

- 2 cups of low-fat white yogurt
- 1 big-size avocado
- 1 cup of sliced banana
- 2 tsp of sliced almonds

Nutritional Values:

Carb:	16 Gr.
Proteins:	13 Gr.
Fats:	20 Gr.

Steps for Cooking:

1. As the first operation for this anti-inflammatory dessert, peel and pit the avocado. So, rinse the pulp under running water, and split it into some slices.
2. Wash and dry the banana slices too.
3. Put the 2 cups of yoghurt in two bowls and then alternately put the banana slices and avocado on top.
4. Sprinkle with the sliced almonds and serve.

Blood Orange Blackberries Fruit Salad

Preapering	Servings	Fridge	Calories
15 Minutes	2 People	0 Minutes	160

Ingredients:

- 1 blood orange
- 1 cup of blackberries
- 8 sliced almonds
- ¼ cup of coconut milk
- 1 tsp of honey

Steps for Cooking:

1. Start by washing and drying the blood orange, so grate its zest and split the pulp into slices.
2. Wash the blackberries too, then drain.
3. Put the just-washed blackberries and oranges in a bowl.
4. Meanwhile, in a small bowl mix the coconut milk and honey and then sprinkle the oranges and blackberries with this emulsion.
5. Stir gently and then transfer to the fridge for 40 minutes.
6. After 40 minutes, arrange the fruit salad in two bowls, cover them with the grated orange rind and the sliced almonds and serve.

Nutritional Values:

Carb:	6 Gr.
Proteins:	4 Gr.
Fats:	11 Gr.

Cherry & Almond Frozen Yogurt

Preapering	Servings	Fridge	Calories
20 Minutes	2 People	4 Hours	240

Ingredients:

- 2 cups of low-fat white yogurt
- 16 pitted cherries
- ¼ cup of sugar free coconut milk
- 2 tbsp of honey
- 1 tbsp of chopped almonds (divided)

Nutritional Values:

Carb:	27 Gr.
Proteins:	6 Gr.
Fats:	8 Gr.

Steps for Cooking:

1. Start this recipe by placing the 2 cups of yogurt, honey, and sugar free coconut milk in a bowl.
2. So, you should take an immersion blender and use it to mince all these ingredients, until smooth.
3. Arrange the just obtained mixture in a low-side container.
4. So, close this container and place it in the freezer.
5. Let the mixture rest in the freezer for about 3 hours, taking care to mix it every 20/25 minutes.
6. After this time indicated, take out the yogurt mixture from the fridge, divide it into pieces and pour it into the blender.
7. Blend again for 40 seconds, then turn off the blender and distribute the frozen yogurt into two bowls.
8. Add the pitted cherries, sprinkle with chopped almonds and serve.

Grape & Avocado Coconut Smoothie

Preapering	Servings	Cooking	Calories
5 Minutes	2 People	0 Minutes	240

Ingredients:

- ½ avocado
- ½ cup of black grapes
- ½ cup of sugar free coconut milk
- 2 tsp of honey

Nutritional Values:

Carb:	13 Gr.
Proteins:	9 Gr.
Fats:	22 Gr.

Steps for Cooking:

1. First, wash all the black grapes, and cut them into little pieces.
2. Peel the half avocado pulp, pit and divide it into little pieces too.
3. Arrange grapes and avocado pieces, coconut milk, ice and honey, in the blender glass and activate it at maximum speed.
4. So, blend everything until you reach a creamy and homogeneous enough mixture.
5. Serve immediately this avocado and grape smoothie.

Lime & Carrot Turmeric Smoothie

Preapering	Servings	Cooking	Calories
10 Minutes	2 People	0 Minutes	50

Ingredients:

- 4 limes
- 2 tbsp of almond milk
- 2 tsp of honey
- 5 carrots
- 1 tsp of turmeric powder

Nutritional Values:

Carb:	8 Gr.
Proteins:	1 Gr.
Fats:	1 Gr.

Steps for Cooking:

1. As the first step for this anti-inflammatory smoothie, wash the five carrots, peel them, and then grate them finely.
2. Squeeze all the lime juice directly into a blender glass.
3. So, join the carrots, almond milk and turmeric powder with the lime juice.
4. So, turn on the blender and work until the carrots are completely minced.
5. Pour the anti-inflammatory carrot and turmeric smoothie into two glasses and serve.

Mango & Pear Turmeric Milkshake

Preapering	Servings	Cooking	Calories
15 Minutes	2 People	0 Minutes	90

Ingredients:

- 1 mango
- 1 ripe pear
- 1 cup of sugar-free almond milk
- 1 tsp of turmeric powder

Nutritional Values:

Carb:	8 Gr.
Proteins:	4 Gr.
Fats:	1 Gr.

Steps for Cooking:

1. So, start this recipe by peeling both the mango and pear, removing the seeds and stone, washing it, and cutting it into pieces.
2. Pour the fruit pieces into the blender glass and mince them for 45 seconds.
3. Now add the turmeric powder and almond milk and blend for another 25 seconds.
4. Now add the ice cubes (the quantity you like more) and mince until you will have a true thick smoothie.
5. Transfer the mango turmeric and pear smoothie into the glasses, add the straws too inside and serve.

Medlar & Pear Honey Lime Syrup Fruit Salad

Preapering	Servings	Cooking	Calories
20 Minutes	2 People	0 Minutes	50

Ingredients:

- 8 pitted medlars
- 1 large pear
- 3 limes
- 1 teaspoon of honey
- 1 tsp of freshly grated ginger

Nutritional Values:

Carb:	15 Gr.
Proteins:	0 Gr.
Fats:	0 Gr.

Steps for Cooking:

1. Wash and dry all the limes, remove the peel and split their pulp into wedges.
2. Peel and wash the pear too, removing the internal seeds and core, then divide it into very small cubes.
3. Wash and pit the medlars, then slice.
4. Prepare the salad fruit syrup: heat a saucepan with 4 tbsp of water, the fresh ginger, the honey and the lime peel.
5. Bring all the syrup ingredients to a boil and reduce them.
6. Switch off, strain the honey and lime syrup and set aside.
7. Put the medlars slices and the pear cubes divided into two bowls for fruit salad, sprinkle them with the honey and lime syrup and let them rest in the fridge until it's time to serve.

Papaya & Orange Cinnamon Smoothie

Preapering	Servings	Cooking	Calories
15 Minutes	2 People	0 Minutes	170

Ingredients:

- 2 oranges
- 1 large papaya
- 1 tsp of ground cinnamon
- 1 cup of low-fat white yogurt

Nutritional Values:

Carb:	32 Gr.
Proteins:	3 Gr.
Fats:	5 Gr.

Steps for Cooking:

1. So, start by peeling the oranges and halve them. Squeeze the juice.
2. Peel the papaya too and divide its pulp into pieces.
3. Put the orange juice and papaya in the blender glass.
4. So, you can add the yogurt and ground cinnamon and activate the blender and blend for 50 seconds/1 minute.
5. Once, done, divide the smoothie between two glasses and serve.

Passion Fruit & Apple Centrifugate

Preapering	Servings	Cooking	Calories
15 Minutes	2 People	0 Minutes	60

Ingredients:

- 2 green ripe apples
- 2 passion fruits

Nutritional Values:

Carb:	12 Gr.
Proteins:	2 Gr.
Fats:	0 Gr.

Steps for Cooking:

1. So, start this recipe by washing the 2 green apples, without removing the peel, and remove the seeds.
2. Do the same with the passion fruits and remove their pulp with the help of a spoon.
3. Cut the apples into chunks.
4. Insert both the fruits in the extractor and, if you don't have one, you can mince everything with the help of a blender.
5. If you decide to use the extractor, the only thing to do is to extract the juice and pour it into two glasses.
6. If you can have only a blender, activate it on and blend until the passion fruits and apples are completely dissolved.
7. So, at this point, you can pass the mixture through a sieve. Done this, filter the juice into two glasses.
8. Add some ice cubes, in case you like more cold juice and serve.

Peach & Ginger Soy Ice Cream

Preapering	Servings	Cooking	Calories
15 Minutes	2 People	0 Minutes	180

Ingredients:

- 7 oz of peach
- 1 tsp of ginger powder
- Half a lemon
- 1 cup of sugar free soy milk
- 2 tbsp of honey

Nutritional Values:

Carb:	20 Gr.
Proteins:	5 Gr.
Fats:	2 Gr.

Steps for Cooking:

1. As first step, peel, pit and cut 1 cup of peaches.
2. Put the peach pieces in the blender glass.
3. Add the soy milk too and blend the ingredients at medium speed.
4. Mince until you get a smooth and homogeneous mixture.
5. Add, at this point, the honey, ginger powder, and the juice of the filtered lemon.
6. Keep on mincing for another minute so that all the ingredients are well incorporated.
7. So, pour the obtained mixture into a container and let rest it in the freezer for an hour.
8. Passed the hour, transfer the mixture to the ice cream maker and, following the time's instruction, prepare your ice cream.
9. Once done, put the peach ginger ice cream back in the freezer and let it harden before serving.

Pear & Yogurt Smoothie

Preapering	Servings	Cooking	Calories
10 Minutes	2 People	0 Minutes	110

Ingredients:

- 1 large pear
- 1/3 cup of low-fat white yogurt
- 8 ice cubes
- ½ cup of sugar free coconut milk

Nutritional Values:

Carb:	22 Gr.
Proteins:	5 Gr.
Fats:	4 Gr.

Steps for Cooking:

1. The first step for this recipe: peel the pear, wash it, cut it into cubes and put it in the blender.
2. Add the low-fat yogurt, coconut milk, and eight ice cubes.
3. So, turn on the blender and work the ingredients until you obtain a creamy and thick smoothie.
4. Pour the pear and coconut smoothie into two glasses and serve.

Pineapple & Banana Shake

Preapering	Servings	Cooking	Calories
5 Minutes	2 People	0 Minutes	210

Ingredients:

- 1 banana
- ½ cup of pineapple pulp
- 1 cup of sugar-free soy milk

Nutritional Values:

Carb:	38 Gr.
Proteins:	2 Gr.
Fats:	3 Gr.

Steps for Cooking:

1. Start with peeling and taking the pineapple fruit pulp, so split it into little pieces.
2. So, proceed with the recipe by peeling and slicing the banana as well.
3. Put pineapple fruit and banana pieces together with the soy milk.
4. Turn on the appliance so you will obtain a smooth and homogeneous enough mixture.
5. Pour the banana and pineapple soy shake into two glasses and serve with a straw.

Pomegranate Berries & Grape Juice

Preapering	Servings	Cooking	Calories
15 Minutes	2 People	0 Minutes	90

Ingredients:

- 2 pomegranates
- 1/3 cup of white grape
- ½ cup of raspberries
- 1 tsp fresh grated ginger
- 2 tsp of honey

Nutritional Values:

Carb:	21 Gr.
Proteins:	2 Gr.
Fats:	0 Gr.

Steps for Cooking:

1. As the first step takes all the grapes and wash them together with raspberries.
2. Cut the pomegranates in horizontally half and divide them into two round slices.
3. Cut the pomegranate slices into wedges and put them in a mixer.
4. Squeeze the remaining pomegranate and strain the juice into the mixer.
5. So, add the grapes, raspberries honey, ginger and a cup of water and blend well.

Purslane & Carrot Coriander Juice

Preapering	Servings	Cooking	Calories
5 Minutes	2 People	0 Minutes	50

Ingredients:

- ½ cup of purslane leaves
- Half a carrot
- The juice of half a lime
- 1 tbsp of honey
- 1 tsp of chopped coriander

Nutritional Values:

Carb:	10 Gr.
Proteins:	1 Gr.
Fats:	0 Gr.

Steps for Cooking:

1. Start by washing all purslane leaves, drying them and placing directly in the mixer.
2. Also wash, dry and split the carrot into large pieces and arrange the mixer too.
3. Now add 1 cup of water, lime juice, chopped coriander and honey, so turn on the mixer and mince all the ingredients at maximum speed.
4. Stir with the help of a spatula.
5. Pour the carrot and purslane juice into two glasses and serve.

Spinach Curry Pine Nuts Extract

Preapering	Servings	Cooking	Calories
15 Minutes	2 People	0 Minutes	140

Ingredients:

- 1 cup of blood orange wedges
- 1 cup spinach leaves
- 2 tsp of pine nuts
- 1 tsp of curry powder

Nutritional Values:

Carb:	22 Gr.
Proteins:	4 Gr.
Fats:	3 Gr.

Steps for Cooking:

1. First step for this recipe: peel, wash and cut the orange in wedges.
2. Put orange wedges, drained spinach leaves in a juicer or centrifuge and extract the juice in a bowl.
3. Now join the curry powder to the juice and mix thoroughly.
4. Arrange the just obtained juice in two glasses, add a few ice cubes, chopped pine nuts and serve.

Strawberry Pink Grapefruit & Ginger Smoothie

Preapering	Servings	Cooking	Calories
10 Minutes	2 People	0 Minutes	100

Ingredients:

- 2 pink grapefruits
- 1 cup of strawberry
- 1 tbsp of grated fresh ginger
- 1 tbsp of honey

Nutritional Values:

Carb:	20 Gr.
Proteins:	3 Gr.
Fats:	0 Gr.

Steps for Cooking:

1. As first step for this recipe, remove the stalk and wash the strawberries, then wash and divide them into some pieces.
2. So, squeeze the pink grapefruit juice into the blender glass.
3. Add the strawberry pieces, honey, and fresh minced ginger.
4. Turn on the blender and mince until the ingredients are completely dissolved.
5. Pour the strawberry and pink grapefruit smoothie into two glasses and serve.

MEAL PLAN

	Breakfast	Snack	Lunch	Snack	Dinner
Day 1	1 cup of sugar-free soy milk, 3 whole grain rusks	Apple and peach cashew milkshake page 82	Alaska Pollock and pumpkin soup page 22, 1 slice of wholemeal bread, 7 oz of veggies	Pineapple and banana shake page 97	Avocado and porcini mushrooms halibut page 34, 7 oz of veggies, 2 oz of brown rice
Day 2	1 cup of green tea, 1 banana, 5 almond	Strawberry pink grapefruit and ginger smoothie page 101	Chia seeds and mustard plaice page 36, 3.5 of legumes soup	3.5 oz of strawberries	Carrot and peas turkey page 38, 7 oz of salad
Day 3	1 cup of sugar-free almond milk, 3 whole grain rusks	3.5 oz of berries, 1 wholemeal rusk	Coconut milk and yellow tomato chicken page 40, 7 oz of veggies, 1 slice of wholemeal bread	Pear and yogurt smoothie page 96	Cauliflower, pink pepper and ginger salmon page 39, 2 oz of black rice
Day 4	1 cup of green tea, 2 wholemeal rusks, 5 almonds	½ cup of low-fat yogurt, 5 almonds	Fennel seeds and asparagus Alaska Pollock cubes page 41, 1 slice of wholemeal bread, 7 oz of green salad	2 pears	Coriander and onion tuna page 42, 7 oz of veggies, 2 oz of black rice

	Breakfast	Snack	Lunch	Snack	Dinner
Day 5	1 cup of sugar free almond milk, 2 wholemeal biscuits, 1 banana	Spinach curry pine nuts extract page 100, 3 walnuts	Fenugreek seeds and marjoram mackerel page 43, 2 oz of black rice, 7 oz of grilled veggies	Passion fruit and apple centrifugate page 94	Zucchini and oat creamy soup page 33, Cucumber and soy basil sauce hake page 44
Day 6	1 glass of citrus juice, 1 omelet, and 5 raspberries	Pomegranat e berries and grape juice page 98, 5 pistachios	Green beans and zucchini chicken pag 46, 2 oz of black rice	3.5 oz of peaches	Mushroom and tofu stuffed cod fillet page 47, 1 slice of wholemeal bread, 7 oz of veggies
Day 7	2 scrambled eggs, ½ avocado	Pear and yogurt smoothie page 96, e pecans	Pecans and cucumber crusted salmon page 48, 2 oz of black rice, 7 oz of salad	Papaya and orange cinnamon smoothie page 93	Pineapple and soy cheese chicken skewers page 50, 1 slice of wholemeal bread, 7 oz of grilled peppers
Day 8	1 cup of sugar-free soy milk, 3.5 oz of blueberries	Banana and cherries fruits bowl page 60	Cinnamon, turmeric and squid soup page 28, 2 oz of black rice, 7 oz of veggies	Medlar and strawberry yogurt cup page 92	Porcini and ginger soy cheese curry page 30, 7 oz of salad, 1 slice of wholemeal bread
Day 9	2 scrambled eggs, ½ avocado and 1 tomato	Flaxseeds mango and apricot bowl page 62	Scallops and chili pepper sauce penne page 31, Radicchio and roasted turkey eggs page 35	Banana pistachio chips page 85	Salmon spinach and peach poke bowl page 54, 7 oz of grilled veggies

	Breakfast	Snack	Lunch	Snack	Dinner
Day 10	1 glass of citrus juice, 1 spinach omelet	Strawberry and pineapple ginger popsicles page 65	Sage and beet greens chipotle crusted cod page 53, 7 oz of veggies, 1 slice of wholemeal bread	Banana and avocado almond yogurt page 86	Soy cheese and jalapeno turkey meatloaf, page 55, 7 oz of veggies, 2 oz of black rice
Day 11	1 cup of green tea, 2 wholemeal rusks, 5 cherries	3.5 oz of banana	Squash and zucchini orange turkey page 56, 1 slice of wholemeal bread, 7 oz of green salad	3.5 oz of strawberries	White zucchini and chicken spicy soup page 58, 1 slice of wholemeal bread, 7 oz of veggies
Day 12	1 glass of orange juice, 1 omelet	½ cup of Greek yogurt, 5 cherries	Pistachio and ginger hake fillet page 51, 7 oz of vegetables 2 oz of brown rice	3.5 of pineapple	Apple and mushroom stuffed chipotle lettuce page 67, 7 oz of grilled cod, 1 slice of wholemeal bread
Day 13	2 scrambled eggs, ½ avocado	Blood orange blackberries fruit salad page 87, 1 wholemeal rusk	Baked soy cheese artichokes page 68, 7 oz of green salad, 1 slice of bread	Cherry and almond frozen yogurt page 88	Avocado and turkey Garam Masala soup page 24, 1 slice of whole meal bread, 7 oz of mixed salad
Day 14	1 toast with turkey and avocado, 1 cup of green tea	Grape and avocado coconut smoothie page 89	Almond and pecans carrot cream page 23, 2 oz of black rice, 5.2 oz of baked turkey	3.5 oz of cherries	Cabbage and radicchio turmeric soup page 25, 5.2 oz of grilled chicken, 1 slice of wholemeal bread.

	Breakfast	Snack	Lunch	Snack	Dinner
Day 15	Chipotle and cilantro scrambled eggs page 61, 1 cup of green tea	Flaxseeds mango and apricot bowl page 62	Cannellini beans and hake soup page 26, 7 oz of veggies	Medlar and strawberry yogurt cup page 63	Chickpea chili turkey cream soup page 27, 7 oz of veggies
Day 16	1 cup of sugar-free soy milk, 2 whole grain rusks, 2 tsp of honey	Rosemary almonds and soy cheese canapés page 64	Cinnamon, turmeric and squid soup page 28, 7 oz of veggies, 1 slice of wholemeal bread	Strawberry and pineapple ginger popsicles page 65	Black cabbage and almond trout stew page 35, 7 oz of veggies, 2 oz of brown rice
Day 17	1 toast with salmon and avocado, 1 cup of green tea	Zucchini and soy cheese jalapeno nuggets page 66	Lentils and tilapia soup page 29, 7 oz of veggies, 1 slice of wholemeal bread	Apple and peach cashew milkshake page 82	Chia seeds and mustard plaice Page 36, 7 oz of veggies, 2 oz of black rice
Day 18	2 scrambled eggs, ½ avocado	Apricot and hazelnuts coconut page 83	Avocado and porcini mushrooms halibut page 34, 7 oz of grilled vegetables, 1 slice of wholemeal bread	Avocado kiwi and banana smoothie page 84	Chipotle and roasted chicken stuffed avocado page 37, 2 oz of black rice, 7 oz of baked vegetables
Day 19	1 glass of orange juice, 1 tomato omelet	Banana pistachio chips page 85	Porcini and ginger soy cheese curry page 30, 7 oz of vegetables, 1 slice of wholemeal bread	Banana and avocado almond yogurt page 86	Carrot and peas turkey page 38, 7 oz of baked vegetables, 2 oz of black rice

	Breakfast	Snack	Lunch	Snack	Dinner
Day 20	1 cup of green tea, 2 wholemeal rusks, 5 strawberries	Blood orange blackberries fruit salad page 87	Cauliflower, pink pepper and ginger salmon page 39, 1 slice of wholemeal bread, 7 oz of green salad	Cherry and almond frozen yogurt page 88	Coconut milk and yellow tomato chicken page 40, 1 slice of wholemeal bread, 7 oz of grilled tomatoes
Day 21	1 cup of sugar-free soy milk, 1 banana	Grape and avocado coconut smoothie page 89	Scallops and chili pepper sauce penne page 31, 7 oz of vegetables, 7 oz of baked cod	Lime and carrot turmeric smoothie page 90	Fennel seeds and asparagus Alaska Pollock cubes page 41, 2 oz of black rice, 7 oz of baked veggies
Day 22	1 toast with tuna and avocado, 1 cup of green tea	Mango and pear turmeric milkshake page 91	Coriander and onion tuna page 42, 2 oz of brown rice, 7 steamed carrots	Medlar and pear honey lime syrup fruit salad page 92	Fenugreek seeds and marjoram mackerel page 43, 7 oz of baked vegetables, 1 slice of wholemeal bread
Day 23	1 cup of sugar-free soy milk, 3.5 oz of raspberries	Papaya and orange cinnamon smoothie page 93	Turmeric and pistachio chicken brown rice page 32, 7 oz of grilled salmon, 7 oz of green salad	Passion fruit and apple centrifugate page 94, 5 almonds	Cucumber and soy basil sauce hake page 44, 7 oz of avocado salad, 1 slice of wholemeal bread

	Breakfast	Snack	Lunch	Snack	Dinner
Day 24	2 scrambled eggs with mushrooms ½ avocado	Peach and ginger soy ice cream page 95	Garam Masala and almond milk tuna page 45, 7 oz of steamed green beans, 1 slice of wholemeal bread	Pear and yogurt smoothie page 96	Green beans and zucchini chicken page 46, 7 oz of green salad, 2 oz of black rice
Day 25	1 glass of orange juice, 1 herbs omelet	Pineapple and banana shake page 97	Zucchini and oat creamy soup page 33, 7 oz of grilled peppers	Pomegranate berries and grape juice page 98	Pecans and cucumber crusted salmon page 48, 7 oz of baked vegetables, 2 oz of black rice
Day 26	1 cup of green tea, 2 wholemeal rusks, 3.5 oz of blackberries	Purslane and carrot coriander juice page 99, 5 pistachios	Mushroom and tofu stuffed cod fillet page 47, 7 oz of baked vegetables, 1 slice wholemeal bread	Strawberry pink grapefruit and ginger smoothie page 101	Pepper and tomato salmon page 49, 7 oz grilled vegetables, 1 slice of wholemeal bread
Day 27	1 glass of citrus juice, 1 omelet, 5 cherries	Spinach curry pine nuts extract page 100, 3 walnuts	Pineapple and soy cheese chicken skewers page 50, 7 oz of green salad, 2 oz of black rice	Apple and peach cashew milkshake page 82	Pistachio and ginger hake fillet page 51, 7 oz of steamed vegetables, 2 oz of black rice
Day 28	1 cup of sugar-free soy milk, 2 whole grain rusks, 2 tsp of honey	Avocado kiwi and banana smoothie page 84	Radicchio and roasted turkey eggs page 52, 1 slice of wholemeal bread, 7 oz of grilled vegetables	Banana and avocado almond yogurt page 86	Sage and beet greens chipotle crusted cod page 53, 2 oz of black rice, 2 oz of baked vegetables

Attention All Food Enthusiasts and Aspiring Chefs!

If you're looking to spice up your cooking game, look no further than Livia McDaniel's latest masterpiece, the "Wok Cookbook".

This cookbook is packed with mouth-watering recipes that are easy to follow and guaranteed to impress your family and friends.

Don't miss out on the opportunity to elevate your culinary skills and explore the endless possibilities of wok cooking. With Livia's expert guidance, you'll learn everything from classic stir-fry dishes to lesser-known regional delicacies.

Order your copy of the Wok Cookbook today and embark on a delicious journey that will leave your taste buds begging for more. Trust us, your kitchen (and stomach) will thank you!

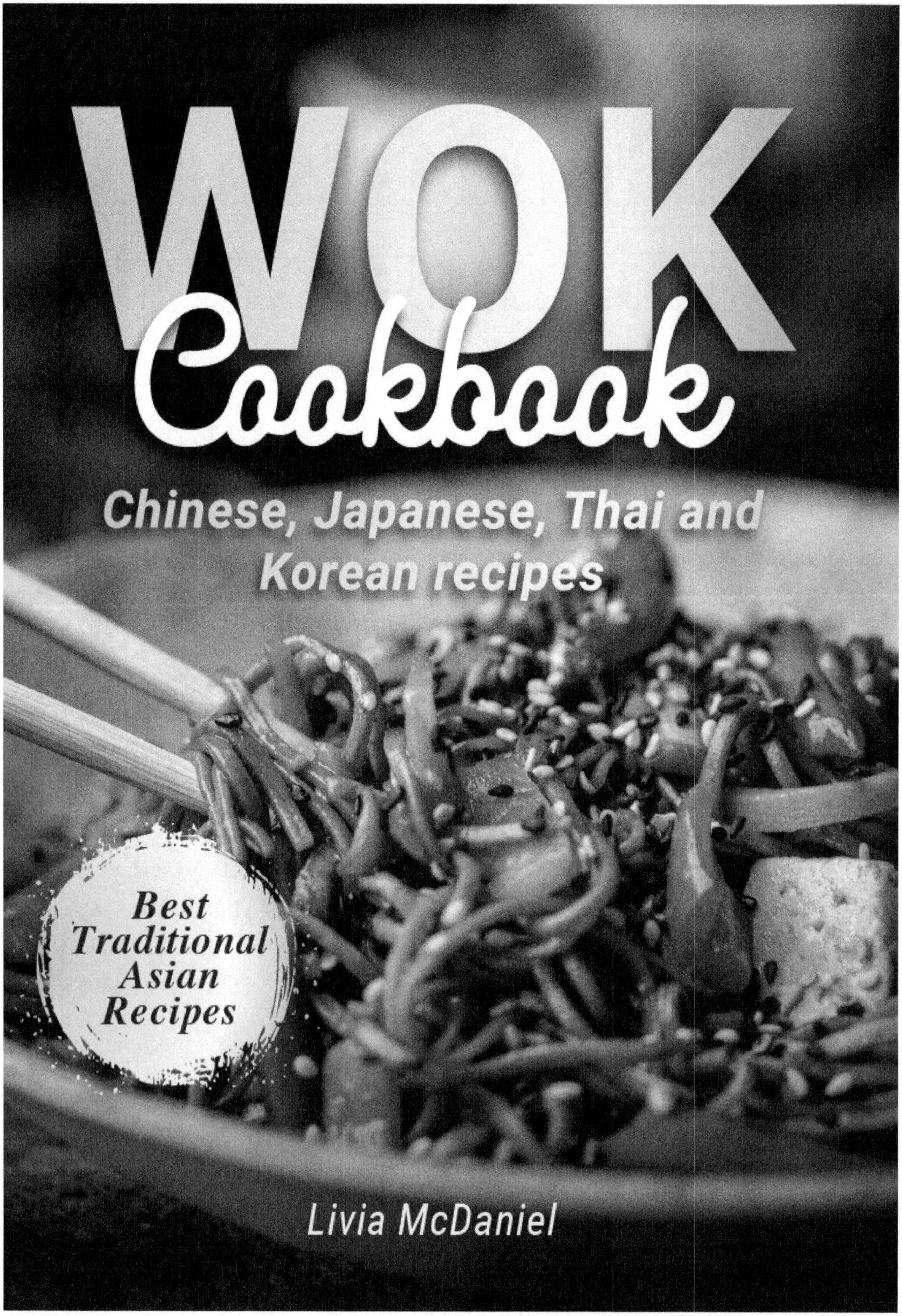
WOK
Cookbook
Chinese, Japanese, Thai and Korean recipes
Best Traditional Asian Recipes
Livia McDaniel

Printed in Great Britain
by Amazon

21737338R00066